LEARN TO PLAY THE
Guitar

A STEP-BY-STEP GUIDE

LEARN TO
PLAY THE
Guitar

A STEP-BY-STEP GUIDE

NICK FREETH

p

This is a Parragon Book

This edition published in 2006

Parragon
Queen Street House
4 Queen Street
Bath BA1 1HE, UK

Copyright © Parragon Books Ltd 2004

ISBN: 1-40547-622-2 (Hardback)

A copy of the CIP data for this book is available
from the British Library upon request.

The rights of Nick Freeth to be identified as the
author of this work have been asserted in
accordance with Section 77 of the Copyright,
Designs and Patents Act of 1988.

Created, designed, produced and packaged by
Stonecastle Graphics Ltd

Designed by Paul Turner and Sue Pressley
Edited by Philip de Ste. Croix
Cover by Talking Design

Photography by Roddy Paine

Printed and bound in China

Pictures on pages 80-81 kindly supplied by
Yamaha-Kemble Music (U.K.) Ltd

With thanks to Dave Cook of Abbey Music,
Tunbridge Wells, Kent for kindly supplying
guitars and equipment for photography.

Contents

Introduction

In the mid-1980s, with the charts and airwaves full of synthesized music, and some of the world's leading fretted instrument makers on the brink of bankruptcy, many doom-laden critics and pundits proclaimed that the guitar would never regain its lost domination over rock and pop.

Thankfully, their predictions proved to be wide of the mark. Combined sales of acoustics and electrics have tripled over the last decade; in 2003, Americans alone spent nearly $500 million on them, and the guitar is currently enjoying a similar resurgence in Britain, where it attracts tens of thousands of new players – of whom you're the very latest! – each year.

Most beginners buy their first 'axe' after months or even years of gazing at guitars in magazines or shop windows, and imagining themselves effortlessly wowing audiences with one. No other instrument generates such intense levels of passion and obsession, or inspires devotees who can't actually play to indulge in anything like the bizarre antics of 'air guitarists': there have never been any reported cases of, say, 'air piano' or 'air percussion'! Sadly, though, fantasy and reverie aren't enough to get a real-life guitar (as opposed to an imaginary one) to produce the music of

your dreams. Hard work and regular practice are needed as well; and during the lengthy process of trying to master the instrument, it's all too easy to become demoralized, and to lose sight of the burning enthusiasm that persuaded you to take it up in the first place.

Learn To Play The Guitar aims to take some of this discouraging sting and slog out of achieving basic competence on acoustic or electric instruments. Its instructions, diagrams and illustrations will guide you through everything from purchasing a guitar and tuning it up to strumming and fingering notes and chords, and performing simple tunes. No previous knowledge is assumed, and the book's upbeat, positive approach will keep you stimulated and focused as you gain the technical and musical skills you require. There's also information about effects pedals, recording gear, and other accessories that you may want to buy now – or a little later – when you start performing with friends or onstage.

Good luck, and have fun as you read and practise!

Chapter 1

Buying a Guitar

Thanks to hi-tech manufacturing methods and cut-throat competition, first-time purchasers seeking reasonably priced, good quality guitars are currently spoiled for choice. Tinny-sounding beginners' instruments with warped fingerboards and strings as thick as piano wire are now largely things of the past, while today's compact, electronically sophisticated amplifiers are a far cry from the overweight, squealing, occasionally exploding practice combos that were all too common just a generation ago.

Nevertheless, the old adage 'let the buyer beware' still holds true when shopping for a guitar. It's essential to decide in advance what sort of acoustic or electric 'axe' you want, to set an overall budget for your purchase, and to obtain preliminary advice not only from interested parties such as salespersons, but also from guitar-playing friends, magazines, websites – and, of course, this book. Choose your guitar store carefully, too: it's worth travelling some distance to find one with substantial stocks, knowledgeable, patient staff, and the peace and relative quiet you'll need when selecting your guitar and amp.

What's Out There?

*You've decided you want to play the guitar – but what sort of guitar?
There's a bewildering variety of instruments on the market at a wide range of
prices; find out more about them here, and you'll be in a good position to
choose which type is right for you and your musical ambitions.*

If you'd like to be able to use your guitar anywhere – indoors or outdoors – with a minimum of fuss, an **acoustic** model will fill the bill. As these have hollow wooden bodies to project their sound, they don't require external electronics like amplifiers and loudspeakers to be heard. The cheapest acoustics are so-called **'classical'** or **'Spanish'** guitars, with nylon strings. They tend to lack the bright sound and powerful tone that's needed for most pop and rock, and we won't be featuring them in detail in this book. Steel-strung **flat-top** instruments are usually a little dearer, but are great for vigorous strumming with a plectrum, or more intricate solo work; in fact, they're probably the most versatile and user-friendly of all guitars, and if you select one that's well constructed and sounds good, it'll give you years of playing pleasure.

If you want to 'rock out', though, there's no substitute for an **electric** guitar. Some have bodies that produce small amounts of acoustic sound, while other 'solid' models like the one shown here have no resonating cavities – but all of them are fitted with electromagnetic **pickups**, which create a rich, sustained tone by converting vibrations from the instrument's steel strings into tiny alternating currents. Pickups in different positions (like

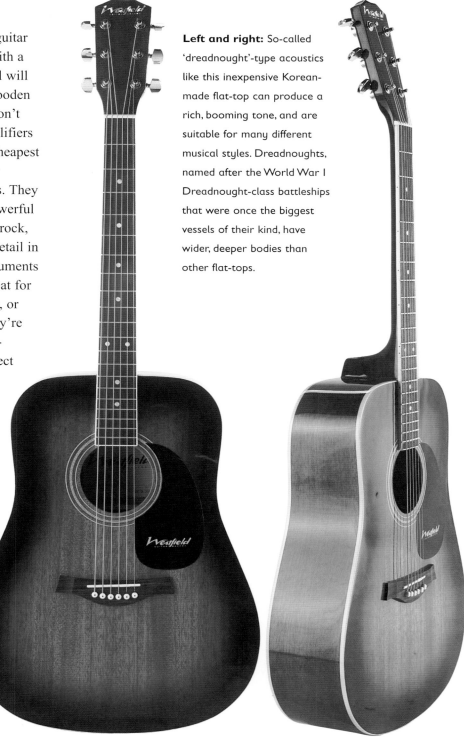

Left and right: So-called 'dreadnought'-type acoustics like this inexpensive Korean-made flat-top can produce a rich, booming tone, and are suitable for many different musical styles. Dreadnoughts, named after the World War I Dreadnought-class battleships that were once the biggest vessels of their kind, have wider, deeper bodies than other flat-tops.

Left: A mid-price flat-top, ideal for a beginner or an intermediate-level player. It boasts a solid-wood top (see pages 14-15), as well as an elegant 'natural' finish and attractive inlays.

Left and right: The Fender Stratocaster — one of the most popular and widely copied of all electric guitar designs. Its contoured body makes it exceptionally comfortable to play. The Stratocaster has three pickups (the lowest of these is slightly angled to boost its treble response), and a double-cutaway body giving easy access to its maple fingerboard.

the three units fitted to the Fender Stratocaster seen here) generate subtly varying blends of treble and bass; their signals are selected, combined and modified by the guitar's switches and controls, then fed to a separate amplifier to be boosted. On the way, they can be fed through effects circuitry to add artificial reverberation, distortion, chorusing, delays and other electronic 'treatments', before being delivered to a loudspeaker that blasts them into the air as soundwaves.

The musical impact of playing an electric is unforgettable, but to experience it, you need to buy an amp and speaker as well as the guitar itself…and to practise in a room with enough insulation to prevent family and neighbours being driven crazy by your efforts!

Acoustic or Electric?

The basic left- and right-hand techniques used to play acoustic and electric guitars are identical; and though some electrics have slightly heavier bodies, there's no significant difference in the amount of physical strength needed to master either type of instrument. So when you make your choice between them, the deciding factors should simply be your own musical preferences and practical requirements.

An acoustic may be taken out of its case (or from beside your bed or chair) and played straight away, without the hassle of plugging into an amplifier. It's perfect for accompanying singers, and its portability can give you music wherever you go; it's even possible to buy 'travel guitars' compact enough to fit in a corner of your car boot, or to qualify as 'carry-on' airline baggage. Standard 'flat-tops' are, of course, a little larger than this, ranging from 'parlour' and so-called 'orchestral' models to the broad-shouldered 'dreadnoughts' and 'jumbos' favoured by folkies and country pickers. All are capable of filling a room with rich, vibrant sound; and some feature onboard electronics that can be connected to an amplifier or public address system to boost their volume further.

As we've already discovered, electric guitars are virtually useless without amplification; they also have a tendency to drown out 'unplugged' instruments and singers. However, in combination with their

Centre and left: The Martin Backpacker, a 'travel guitar' designed by the C.F. Martin company of Nazareth, Pennsylvania. Despite its size and unconventional body shape, it produces a clear, though relatively soft tone. The Backpacker's overall dimensions — 33in (84cm) long and just 2in (5cm) deep — are much smaller than those of a regular flat-top. However, its standard-width fingerboard makes it easy to play.

Far left: An acoustic with a secret...the Backpacker has a built-in electronic pickup, which can be plugged into an amplifier via the jack socket concealed in one of its strap buttons.

amps, they offer a far more extensive tonal palette than any acoustic. Warm, mellow chords can be transformed into rasping funk or screaming distortion at the flick of a switch, and even more dramatic effects are available with the aid of a built-in 'whammy bar' (a mechanical device that 'detunes' the strings, causing pitch bends) or external pedal units. An electric can sound quiet and restrained as well, but its potential for wild, over-the-top showmanship – reflected in the bold, and sometimes downright weird body shapes and colours of many models – is always there…and if such characteristics appeal to you, then you shouldn't hesitate to buy one!

Below: The Fender Stratocaster's spring-loaded vibrato system, controlled by a metal arm nicknamed a 'whammy bar', can produce dramatic pitch bends on notes and chords.

Left and right: A budget-priced, Far-Eastern-built solid-body electric with a single cutaway. Signals from its two pickups can be mixed and adjusted using the volume and tone controls on the lower right of the instrument's top.

Left: Electric guitars can be surprisingly heavy; always use a strong strap when you play standing up!

Choosing Your 'Axe'

As you still know comparatively little about guitars, purchasing one can be a risky undertaking! Listen carefully to what knowledgeable friends, shop assistants, and other reliable sources have to say on the subject, but also take account of your own 'gut instinct' when trying out an instrument. Even the most highly recommended model won't satisfy you if it 'feels' wrong when it's in your hands.

If you're going for an acoustic guitar, buy a steel-strung flat-top rather than a nylon-strung classic, for the reasons explained earlier. The cheapest acoustics are made from laminated timbers, and can sound quite reasonable; however, for better tone, select one with a solid (non-laminated) top. More expensive models boast tops, backs and sides constructed entirely from solid woods.

Electric guitars tend to be trickier to choose. Several manufacturers offer their most famous models in both 'premium' and 'budget' versions, and there's little visual difference (though a considerable sonic one!) between (say) an American-made Fender Stratocaster costing over £1000, and the 'Squier' rendition of the same design, mass-produced under licence in China, and retailing for a fifth of this price. Go for the best-built and richest sounding electric you can afford, and avoid instruments laden with complicated vibratos and other 'bells and whistles'; axes with simpler specifications will prove more durable and better value.

Whether you're looking for an acoustic or an electric, get the salesperson or a guitar-savvy friend to demonstrate it by playing single notes and chords at various pitches and fingerboard positions. Then try it out for yourself: place its body on your right

Left: It's easiest to play when you're sitting down, and your guitar should always feel well balanced and comfortable in this position. If it seems unwieldy or too heavy for you, put it aside and choose another one!

thigh, put your left hand on its neck, and assess it for balance and comfort. Next, strum its strings from bottom to top with your right-hand index finger: the six notes should be equal in volume, and produce a ringing, sustained sound, with no rattles or buzzes. Finally, check for cracks, bad scratches and other damage – before repeating the whole process on two or three other 'shortlisted' axes. The instrument with the best performance and strongest overall appeal is the one to buy!

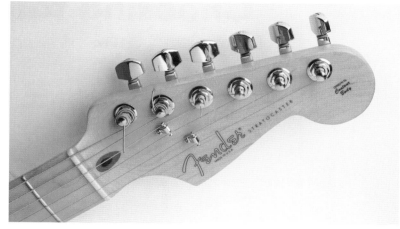

Above: Check out the tuning keys on your shortlisted guitars: do they turn smoothly, and are they free of dirt, corrosion and discoloration?

Far left: Even as a beginner, you can get a reasonable idea of an instrument's capabilities – and find out whether it suits you – simply by holding it and strumming it.

Left: When trying out a guitar with a strap, ensure that the instrument doesn't hang down too low. This 'Les Paul'-style axe should be raised by a couple of inches for optimum comfort.

Choosing Your Amp

When choosing an amp, it's worth taking time to ensure that it's well matched to your guitar, and capable of working in harmony with it to produce the musical results you're seeking.

After spending hundreds of pounds on their instruments, some budding electric guitarists treat the purchase of an amplifier almost as an afterthought. Such an approach is likely to lead to disappointment and frustration, as the amp and loudspeaker are the axe's sonic 'delivery system', and can obscure or destroy all its treasured tonal qualities if they aren't up to the job.

The biggest selling and most practical form of guitar amplifier is the 'combo' – a single, fairly light, easily transportable box containing both the 'amp' itself (the electronics that boost the current from the guitar's pickups to usable levels) and one or more loudspeakers. (Separate amps and speaker cabinets, known as 'stacks' and popular with stadium rockers, are less than ideal for domestic use!) Combos range in quality, size and price from modest practice units costing under £100 to heavyweight professional models designed to withstand the rigours of life 'on the road'. Though you don't need one of these monsters at present, you should be careful to select a combo that will operate reliably and bring out the best in your guitar. It needs to have an output of no less than 15 watts RMS ('root mean square', a standard form of audio power measurement), and a loudspeaker with a diameter of at least eight inches (20cm). Amps with lower wattages and smaller speakers than this will tend to sound thin and feeble, even in your living room.

Above: With its 30-watt output and 10in (25cm) loudspeaker, this Laney HCM30R solid-state combo amp packs a considerable punch. Its equalization controls (below) allow players to 'shape' their sound.

Cheaper combos usually feature transistorized (solid-state) circuitry. This has a clean, if rather neutral, sound, and requires little maintenance; but many guitarists consider 'tranny' amplifiers inferior to those driven by valves, which boast a warmer, richer tone, and can create velvety overdrive and distortion. Inevitably, such performance comes at a premium: valve amps are more expensive, heavier and more fragile that their solid-state counterparts – but audition one in the shop, and you may find it hard to resist!

Left: When trying out an electric guitar through an amp, switch between its pickups and compare their sounds. The one in the neck ('front') position normally produces a warm, slightly bassy tone, while the bridge ('back') pickup should have a higher-pitched cutting edge.

Left: Don't be afraid to experiment with the amp's controls – and make sure that it sounds good at the low volume settings you're likely to be using at home.

Extra, Extra

*The enticingly packaged accessories surrounding the cash desk in most guitar shops can be as hard to resist as sweets at a supermarket checkout – but only a few of the goodies displayed there are 'must-haves'. These are: a **plectrum**; a **tuning aid** for your new guitar; a **case** or **bag** in which to transport it; and a **lead**, if you're using an electric.*

Plectrums (also known as **picks** or **flat-picks**) come in various shapes, thicknesses and colours, and couple of pounds will buy you a handful of them. As you can't yet be sure which will suit you best, it's worth choosing several different types.

The cheapest available tuning device is a **pitch pipe** made up of six harmonica-style reeds. When blown, these produce the notes to which you set the strings of your guitar. (Some players use a metal **tuning fork** as a pitch reference for a single string, and then adjust the other five strings in relation to it, but we won't be featuring this rather more involved method here.) The easiest – though costliest – way of tuning is with a

Left: A selection of plectrums in slightly varying shapes and thicknesses. The ones shown here are made from plastic.

Above: Pitch pipes are durable, portable... and, unlike more sophisticated tuning devices, they don't require batteries!

battery-powered **electronic tuner**, which 'listens' to your strings through its built-in microphone (it can also be plugged into an electric guitar), and provides a visual indication, via a meter or LCD, as to whether they're correctly pitched, too high, or too low.

Though you may be tempted to carry your new guitar home wrapped in cellophane, or in a cardboard box, it's best to protect it

Right: The pitch pipe's reeds provide the individual notes to which you can tune your guitar's six strings.

Far right: The visual displays on this electronic tuner take the uncertainty — and much of the skill — out of tuning.

from scratches, bumps and the weather with some sort of case. For everyday transportation, a soft, padded **gig bag** should suffice; **hardshell cases**, often made from fibreglass, give much greater protection, but can be very expensive.

Your **electric guitar lead** needs to withstand years of being yanked, stretched, and occasionally trodden on. Select one with a heavy-duty, well insulated cable and robust jack plugs; it should be at least 10 feet (3m) long.

Below: Gig bags like these can be carried by hand or strapped to your back. They provide adequate protection for your guitar on most journeys, but owners of more expensive or delicate instruments should consider investing in a hardshell case.

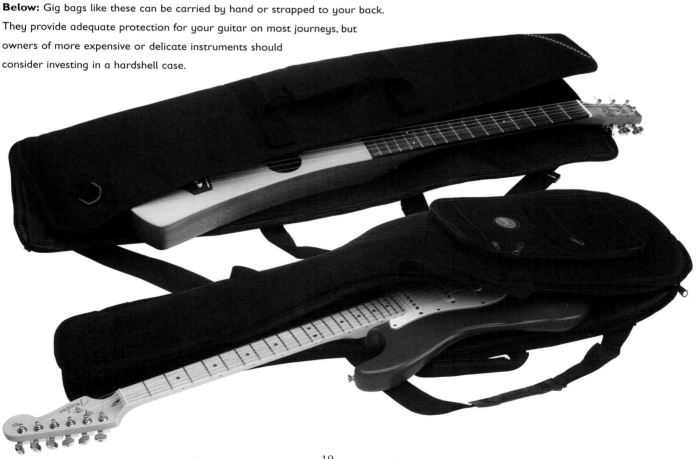

Chapter 2
Getting Started

There's a world of sonic difference between the thundering, overdriven tones of an amped-up axe and the more delicate chords and licks produced by an acoustic guitar. However, the two types of instrument share so many essential similarities that it makes sense, when explaining the basics, to use the same instructions and exercises for both of them; and such an approach is followed in this book. If you're a budding electric picker, you should keep your overall volume, and any 'fuzz' or 'gain' settings on your amplifier, at a fairly low, 'clean' level for general practising purposes ... though you'll obviously want to make occasional experiments (perhaps while your family and neighbours are safely out of earshot!) with louder playing and distortion.

The next few pages show you how to tune your guitar and strike it with a plectrum. Once you've mastered these essentials, you'll be able to progress from simple chords to your first 'proper' tune, *Amazing Grace* — for which you'll learn both the harmonies and the melody.

Tuning Up and Picking

*It's the moment of truth: time to take up your guitar and begin playing!
Start by selecting an upright, armless chair; place a small table in front of it
to rest this book on, and have your plectrum and tuning device within easy
reach. Sit down with the guitar, resting it on your right thigh, and steadying
it with your left hand if necessary.*

Hold the plectrum between your right-hand thumb and index finger, position it over the strings, and sweep it across them, moving downwards (towards the floor) from the thickest to the thinnest. Keep the plectrum straight, allowing only its tip to make contact with the strings, and don't dampen their vibrations with your hands: let the notes ring free. Practise until you can 'strum' the strings smoothly – never mind about the rather non-musical chord you're producing! Then try playing them one-by-one, stopping your plectrum after each stroke to prevent it making accidental contact with adjacent strings.

Once you've mastered this technique, you'll be ready to **tune** your instrument. Its strings, numbered from 6th (the thickest) to 1st (the thinnest), should be set to the following alphabetically named pitches: **E** (6th), **A** (5th), **D** (4th), **G** (3rd), **B** (2nd) and a higher **E** (1st). If you have a pitch pipe, you'll see these numbers and note letters etched near its reed-holes. Put the pipe in your mouth, blow the E/1st reed, and pick the 1st string. Are the two notes identical, or is the string slightly higher or lower than the pipe? To make it match the blown note, use your left hand to adjust the 1st string's **machine head** (see photograph),

Left: Preparing to play. This method of holding the guitar is relaxed and comfortable, and will ensure good balance even if the left hand is removed from the neck.

Left: A single-note pick stroke — only the plectrum's 'arrow-head' tip should actually make contact with the string.

Below left: Tuning up (i): pick the 1st (E) string with the plectrum, and compare the note it produces with the sound from your pitch pipe, or tuner reading.

Below: Tuning up (ii): now turn the string's tuning key, increasing or decreasing the tension until it produces the correct pitch.

tightening or loosening the tension until pipe and string correspond exactly. Repeat the same process for the other five strings, and you'll be in tune!

You may find this process difficult until you develop an 'ear' for pitch differences — but if you're using an electronic tuner, it immediately becomes child's play. Simply set up the tuner according to the manufacturer's instructions, sound each string, and raise or lower it until the unit's meter tells you the frequency is correct!

Above: An electric guitar plugged directly into an electronic tuner.

Your First Chord

*Now you've tuned up, and have learned how to strike the strings, it's time to try playing a **chord** – the term given to a group of notes that make musical 'sense' when they're sounded together.*

Thanks to the way the guitar is tuned, quite a number of basic chords can be created with very little effort. The easiest is known as **E minor** (you'll be discovering how chords are named later on – for now, we'll concentrate on locating and picking them). It contains three essential notes: **E** (which gives the chord its name, and is referred to as its **root**), **G**, and **B**.

If these seem familiar, it's because they correspond to the pitches to which you've just set your guitar's top three strings (G/3rd, B/2nd, and E/1st) – so you can produce a chord of E minor straight away by taking your plectrum and playing the

3rd, 2nd and 1st, without the lower three strings. It may require practice to avoid grazing the 4th string when 'hitting' the 3rd, but you'll soon be able to do this cleanly and accurately; as before, begin by strumming, and then sound the G, B and E more slowly, one after the other.

Though our three open strings provide all the notes for E minor, you may feel that the chord still seems to lack something. The incompleteness is due to the fact that the lowest note (G/3rd string) isn't the root of E minor. The missing root is, of course, E, and we can easily add it to the bottom of our chord by picking the guitar's lowest

Below: Picking the guitar's 3rd string produces the note G – one of the pitches making up the chord of E minor that you're about to play.

Above: The root of our E minor chord comes from the open 6th (E) string. This is the lowest note the guitar can produce in normal tuning.

Left: After sounding the low E, your plectrum should 'miss out' the 5th and 4th strings, and strike the 3rd string (followed by the 2nd and 1st) to complete the chord of E minor.

string (E/6th), and then going on to strike the 3rd, 2nd and 1st as before.

There's now only one remaining problem – the awkward jump the plectrum has to make from the bottom E to the 3rd (G). We can't strum across all six strings, because the pitches of the intervening A and D strings don't 'belong' in an E minor chord. To remedy this, we need to use the left hand to change those notes by **fretting** – which is explained overleaf.

A Full 'E Minor'

*Your left hand has had an easy time of it so far…
but that's about to change, as you start using it
to form notes and chords.*

Before going any further, have a look at its fingernails; they need to be as short as possible, or you'll find it difficult or impossible to hold down the strings. If necessary, take a moment to trim them – then pick up the guitar again, and position your left hand on its neck as shown in the photograph. Place the tip of your **third finger** on the 4th (D) string just below the second of the guitar's frets (counting up from the white block known as the **nut**), press the string down onto the wood of the fretboard, and try picking the 4th string.

Fretting cleanly

Hopefully, you'll be rewarded by a ringing, unmuffled new note – but if there's buzzing, or the string doesn't vibrate at all, adjust the angle and position of your third finger: its top joint should be at 90 degrees to the fretboard, not leaning over or touching adjacent strings, and its tip should be making firm contact with the string. All this may feel uncomfortable at first, but you'll find that your fingertips and hand muscles will soon become accustomed to what you're asking them to do!

Below: Hold down the D string at the 2nd fret with your third finger to produce an E – the bottom note in our four-string E minor chord.

Above: Getting ready to strum a four-string E minor. The chord comprises a fretted E from the 4th string (see opposite), plus G, B and E from the 'open' (unfretted) 3rd, 2nd and 1st strings.

Left: Once you've added a second fretted note (B from the 5th string/2nd fret), you can strum across all six strings to produce a full E minor chord.

Once you've got your fretted 4th string working properly, strum the top four strings and listen to the effect the fingered note (an E) has on your chord of E minor. Now, to make the sound even richer, put the **second finger** of your left hand on the 5th (A) string below the 2nd fret, so that it's 'next door' to your third finger. Press down on the string, get the fretted note (a B, one 'letter' up from the 5th's open A pitch) sounding cleanly, and strum the guitar's six strings, from bottom (6th) to top (1st).

A six-string chord

Congratulations – you've now learned a full chord of E minor! Give your left hand a brief rest; it'll soon be busy holding down new fingerings…

Two More Chords

*Let's investigate some of the other easy chords
that can be produced with a combination of
open and fretted strings.*

G major (also known simply as **G**) consists of a **G** root, plus **B** and **D** – notes that can be found (though not in this order) on the guitar's open 4th, 3rd and 2nd strings. Strum these by themselves, being careful not to let your plectrum touch the 1st string at the end of its stroke. The resultant chord sounds pleasant enough, but could do with some filling out; and, like our open-string E minor, it suffers from not having its root (G) as its bottom or **bass** note. To remedy this, press your second finger onto the 6th string behind the 3rd fret, as shown in the picture, then pick the fretted note on its own. Alter the angle and pressure of your finger as necessary to get a clean sound, and then add a new note, B, from the 5th string by holding it down behind the 2nd

fret with your index finger. Test the two notes for buzzes, ensuring that the second finger isn't catching the side of the 5th string, before strumming from the 6th string

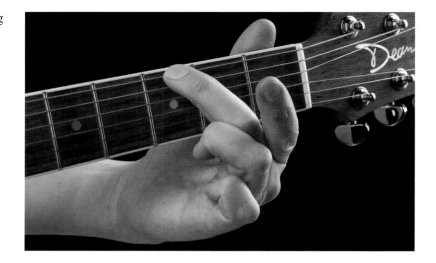

Above: To start building up a six-string G major chord, hold down this G – its bass or root note – on the guitar's 6th string with your second finger.

Left: Adding a B from the 5th string/2nd fret allows you to play a five-note G chord; only the 1st string is omitted when strumming the shape.

to the 2nd. Our G chord is now rich and sonorous, but to make it a six-stringer, we need just one more note – a G from the 3rd fret position on the 1st string, provided by your third finger.

The full G chord will be quite a stretch for your inexperienced left hand; but once you're able to play it, other narrower fingerings, such as the **C major** or **C** chord illustrated opposite, will seem relatively easy! Our new shape comprises a C root from the 5th string/3rd fret, supplied by your third finger, an E from the 4th string/2nd fret (second finger), and a C on the 2nd string/1st fret (index finger). The 3rd and 1st strings are left open, and the bottom E string isn't sounded. Use the photograph as a guide to your finger positions, and keep practising the chord until every note rings true and clear.

Top: The fingering for a full six-string G major, incorporating the fretted 1st string. Note the position of the thumb, which provides support and stability for the other digits.

Above: A five-string chord of C major; its C root is supplied by the 5th string.

A Fourth Chord – and Your First Tune

Learning chords is satisfying, but they aren't much use until you can employ them on real songs and tunes. Over the next few pages, you're going to start doing just that – in fact, by the time you reach the end of this chapter, you'll be able to play a simple melody as well as providing an accompaniment for it.

First, though, you need to master just one more chord – a four-stringer known as **D major** or **D**.

D's root is conveniently located on the open 4th string, and when you strum the chord, you should start your plectrum stroke from there, omitting the 6th and 5th. However, all its other notes have to be fretted: your index finger goes behind the 2nd fret on the 3rd string to make an A, while the third holds down a D (2nd string/3rd fret), and the second presses down the 1st string behind the 2nd fret, creating a so-called 'F sharp'. As always when trying out new shapes, be patient, and don't worry if it takes a while to get the strings sounding properly!

Let's now apply your 'repertoire' of four chords to a proper piece of music: the song *Amazing Grace*, chosen because its familiarity makes it much easier for you to synchronize your finger and plectrum movements to its words and tune. Before embarking on it, spend some time playing your E minor, G, C and D shapes in slow succession, and in various orders; to help you do this, their fingerings are set out in 'grid' form opposite. Once you're able to guide your left-hand digits from shape to shape without too much fumbling and delay, look through the lyrics of *Amazing Grace*, which are printed here with chord

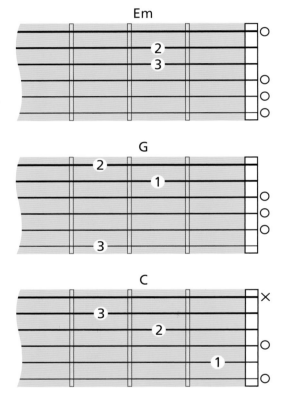

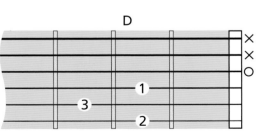

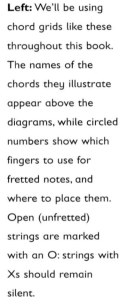

Left: We'll be using chord grids like these throughout this book. The names of the chords they illustrate appear above the diagrams, while circled numbers show which fingers to use for fretted notes, and where to place them. Open (unfretted) strings are marked with an O: strings with Xs should remain silent.

names above them. Try singing the tune very slowly (either out loud, or 'in your head'): do this first without any guitar backing, and then add the chords, playing a single plectrum stroke on each of them. Take as much time as you need between

Left: This D major shape, whose fingering also appears on the grid opposite, is one of the four chords needed to play *Amazing Grace*.

Left: The right hand, seen here in mid-strum. You should use just one plectrum stroke per chord shape for the present.

Below: E minor occurs just twice in *Amazing Grace* – on the words 'wretch' and 'now'.

changes, gradually building up fluency and speed as you gain confidence.

   G   **G**   **C**   **G**
Amazing grace! How sweet the sound,

     G   **Em**   **D**
That saved a wretch like me!

  G   **G**   **C**   **G**
I once was lost, but now am found,

D **G**   **Em D G**
Was blind, but now I see.

You may need to spend several hours practising the version of *Amazing Grace* featured on the previous two pages – but once you can manage the chord changes smoothly and steadily, you'll probably want to make your guitar part a bit more interesting. A good way to achieve this is by increasing the number of plectrum strokes you use while accompanying the tune; until now, you've been sounding each chord just once, but adding extra 'strums' will support the melody better, and help to enliven its overall 'feel'.

The rhythm of *Amazing Grace* contains recurring groups of three beats, each comprising a strong pulse, followed by two slightly weaker ones. The song's opening syllable – the 'A-' of 'Amazing' – is weak; the first strong pulse is on '-ma-', and the succession of strong-weak-weak patterns (musicians call these **bars** or **measures**) continues from here to the end, with the next few strong beats falling on 'grace', 'sweet', 'sound', 'saved', 'wretch', and so on. Why not strum on all three beats,

making the first chord in each group of three a little heavier than the other two? You can do this easily by following the chart below, which sets out the lyrics, beats (with the strong ones **emboldened**), and chord changes for the whole song.

Above: Sounding the bass note for each chord 'solo' at the start of every bar is an old, but effective, guitarist's trick. Here, the plectrum makes contact with the 5th string, providing a root C beneath the words 'sweet' (line **1**) and 'now' (line **3**).

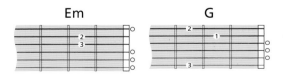
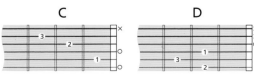

	G			G			C			G		
A-ma	-	zing	grace!	-	How	sweet	-	the	sound,	-	That
3	*1*	*2*	*3*	*1*	*2*	*3*	*1*	*2*	*3*	*1*	*2*	*3*

	G			Em			D			D		
saved	-	a	wretch -		like	me!	-	-			I
1	*2*	*3*	*1*	*2*	*3*	*1*	*2*	*3*	*1*	*2*	*3*

	G			G			C			G		D
once	-	was	lost,	-	but	now	-	am	found,	-	Was
1	*2*	*3*	*1*	*2*	*3*	*1*	*2*	*3*	*1*	*2*	*3*

	G			Em	D	G				
blind,	-	but	now	-	I	see.	-	-	-
1	*2*	*3*	*1*	*2*	*3*	*1*	*2*	*3*	*1*	*2*

Above: After picking an open D, the plectrum continues its downward movement, preparing to strike the top three strings.

Left: When strumming, you may find it easier to sweep the pick across the strings by slightly altering its angle, as shown.

An even more effective method of 'spicing up' your instrumental backing would be to pick just the root or bass note of each specified shape on the first beat of every three-pulse cycle, followed by the full 4-, 5- or 6-string chord on the other two beats; we'll be focusing on this more elaborate kind of plectrum work in Chapter 4.

Having provided a chordal accompaniment for *Amazing Grace*, how about having a go at its melody? To do so, you need to learn how to read **guitar tablature** – an easy-to-master system that shows where the various notes required for songs and tunes lie on the fingerboard.

'Tab' is written on six lines corresponding to the guitar's strings; the lowest line represents the 6th, the one above it the 5th, and so on. Numbers superimposed on these lines indicate that the strings for which the lines stand should be sounded: a zero tells you to play a string open; other digits (from 1 upwards) give the number of the fret position where the string needs to be held down. To see how this works, take a look at the example below: it contains 'tab' notation for the four chords you've been using in *Amazing Grace*.

Above: Having just struck the first two notes of *Amazing Grace's* melody from the unfretted D and G strings, the plectrum heads towards the next one – B, on the open 2nd.

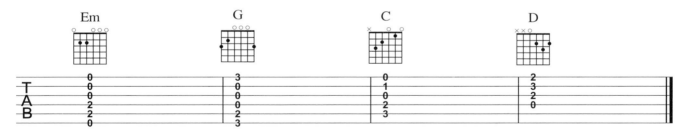

Our second piece of 'tab' sets out a slightly simplified version of the song's melody, plus its lyrics and backing chords; the vertical lines on the stave mark off the three-beat **bars** you learned about earlier. As you can see, the majority of the notes come from open strings, beginning with a D (4th) string on the syllable 'A-'. The first fretted pitch, on 'How', is supplied by the 3rd string, held down at the 2nd position; the recommended left-hand finger to use for this (2) is shown by a small digit above the stave. Other fretted notes are shown similarly, and you'll soon find that locating the correct string to press down and pick will become second nature to you – if you keep practising!

Left: This fretted 4th string E occurs in bars 3, 10 and 11 of the tune; it's played by the second finger at the 2nd fret (see tablature).

Below: The notes for the words 'like me' (bars 6-7) are A (3rd string/2nd fret/second finger) and D (2nd string/3rd fret/third finger). By holding them down together before you pick them, you'll make the melody line sound smoother.

Melody and backing

First of all, try the *Amazing Grace* tune 'solo'; then, either ask a guitar-savvy friend to strum the indicated chords as you perform it, or record them, and use the tape to accompany yourself as you play the melody. If you do this, give a spoken 'count-in' ('1-2-3') on the recording before you strum the first G chord; this will allow you to pick the song's opening D (for the first syllable of 'Amazing') on the '3' beat immediately prior to the chord.

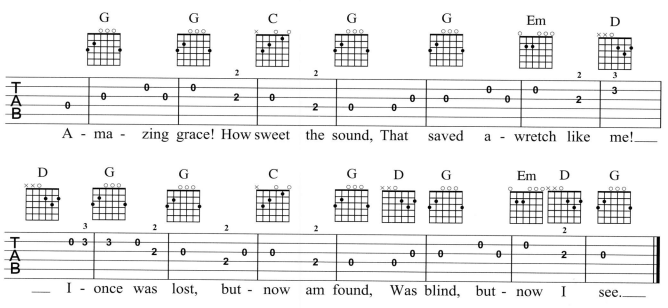

35

Chapter 3

Playing the Blues

Apparently simple, yet emotionally profound and infinitely flexible, blues has its roots in the songs brought from Africa by the first black Americans, but possesses an extraordinary ability to refresh and renew itself, and has been a vital part of almost every major trend in jazz and pop for the last century.

At some stage, all guitarists need to play the blues, and this chapter gives you a crash course in its fundamentals. Featured topics include its 'standard' 12-bar structure (sometimes more honoured in the breach than the observance, as we shall see), and the 'dominant 7th' chords that provide a piquant new flavour to its harmonies. You'll also have the opportunity to try out some simple blues-based riffs and licks – potential building blocks for your future solos and lead parts…

The Basic '12-Bar'

Blues is the most influential style in the history of modern popular music, and its most basic form, the so-called '12-bar', is used in thousands of songs and tunes. Let's begin by playing a very simple version of the '12-bar', featuring three now-familiar chords: G, C and D.

You first read about the concept of bars – groups of strong and weak beats – in the previous chapter. A single verse of a typical blues has (you guessed it!) twelve of them; however, unlike the three-beat measures in *Amazing Grace*, blues bars usually contain four beats: a strong initial one, followed by three weaker pulses (**1**-2-3-4). Here's how they can be combined with chords (each of which should be strummed once on every beat) to make a complete 12-bar blues cycle, with G as its 'home' or 'key' chord:

G	G	G	G
1 2 3 4	*1 2 3 4*	*1 2 3 4*	*1 2 3 4*
C	C	G	G
1 2 3 4	*1 2 3 4*	*1 2 3 4*	*1 2 3 4*
D	C	G	D
1 2 3 4	*1 2 3 4*	*1 2 3 4*	*1 2 3 4*

At the end of the twelfth bar, you can either go back to bar 1 for another 'verse', or conclude by playing a single G chord.

This 12-bar structure – the 'bare bones' of the blues – offers endless scope for additions and modifications. One classic method of changing it is to replace some of its standard chords with 'dominant 7ths', like the G7, C7 and D7 shapes shown in the photographs and diagrams on these pages. Practise these on their own, and then try using them in the revised 12-bar sequence shown on the right; we'll be looking at them more closely on the next few pages.

Above: The top note of the G7 chord, held down at the first fret, is a little lower than the one used for our regular G shape. As you can see from the photograph and diagrams, this small change also involves refingering the chord's other two fretted notes (on the 6th and 5th strings).

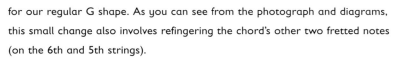

G	G	G	G7
1 2 3 4	*1 2 3 4*	*1 2 3 4*	*1 2 3 4*
C	C7	G	G
1 2 3 4	*1 2 3 4*	*1 2 3 4*	*1 2 3 4*
D7	C7	G	D7
1 2 3 4	*1 2 3 4*	*1 2 3 4*	*1 2 3 4*

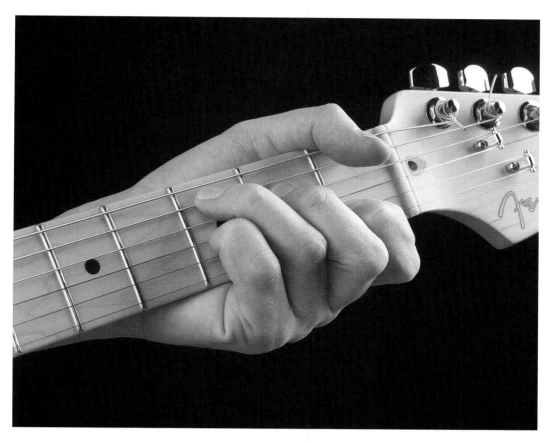

Left: For the C7 shape, the little finger frets the 3rd string at the 3rd fret. The original C chord (see grid below centre) leaves this string open.

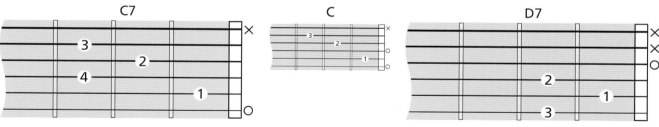

C7   C   D7

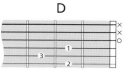

D

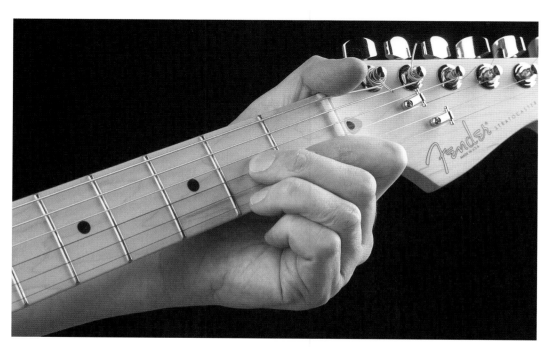

Left: D7 is perhaps the easiest of the three chords in our blues. It owes its distinctive sound to the altered note provided by the 2nd string, which is held down at the 1st fret.

'Dom 7' Chords and Riffs

The three dominant 7th chords you've just learned differ from their respective 'parents' by just one note – though this is enough to give our '12-bar' a welcome injection of blues flavour! It's worth looking at these changes a little more closely:

G/G7

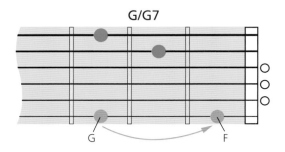

• In G7, the top string note shifts down two frets from G to F.

D/D7

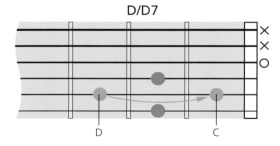

• In D7, the D on the 2nd string/3rd fret is replaced by a C from the 1st fret position of the same string.

C/C7

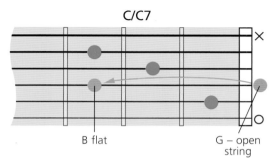

B flat   G – open string

• In C7, the 3rd string, played open in the original C shape, is held down at the 3rd fret to produce a note called **B flat**, which we haven't come across before.

G7, D7, C7 are named 'dominant 7ths' because the 'extra' tones they contain (F, C and B flat) are altered versions of the second-to-last (i.e. seventh) notes in the eight-note **scales** of G, D and C from which the chords themselves are constructed. Their technicalities are explained in depth in more advanced guitar tutors – but for the present we'll stay focused on their practical uses in the blues!

Below: Lick 1 (see tablature). Here, the open 3rd string is combined with notes from the 4th string, fingered by the second and third fingers.

Left: In Lick 2, the second and third fingers 'walk up' the 3rd string, while the 2nd string is held down at the 1st fret.

Left: Lick 3, bar 1. All four left-hand fingers are needed to play the successive notes from the 3rd string's 2nd, 4th, 5th and 4th frets. These are combined with the open 4th string.

Below: The notes and fingering in Lick 3, bar 2 are identical to those for Lick 2.

Now you know which notes form the active ingredients for 'dom 7s', you can start to build simple but effective patterns (often known as **licks** or **riffs**) from them. Three typically 'bluesy' examples are shown here: a two-note G7-based pattern combining the open G (3rd) string with D, E and F from the 4th; a second riff moving towards a 'C7'-type combination of B flat and C on the 3rd and 2nd strings; and a 'D-to-D7' progression played on the 4th and 3rd strings. This trio of licks is set out below in a 12-bar sequence with numbered beats beneath them.

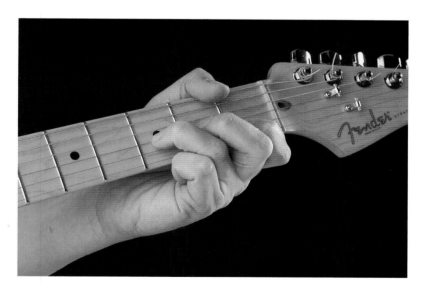

Lick 1

Lick 2

Lick 3

Blues in E Major

*We've had quite a lot of mileage out of our G, C, D and E minor chords – in fact, every exercise so far has featured G major as its starting and finishing point, making G what's known as the **key** for all these pieces. However, there's no reason why we have to restrict ourselves in this way.*

We are free to select any note we fancy as the keynote for our songs and tunes, and to use its associated harmonies to support and enrich them – though our choice of key, and the corresponding need for new or modified chord shapes and fingerings, will obviously have a considerable effect on the nature of the sound we create.

To find out what a key change can do, let's play a blues in E major – a favourite with guitarists, as it allows the instrument to make extensive use of the bass E on its open 6th string. The diagrams opposite give the left-hand positions for the three main chords in E (E, A, and B) and their respective dominant 7ths. Once you've got your fingers around them, try them out in the 12-bar sequence below, strumming on each beat as usual, but ignoring (for the moment) the additional chords printed in italics (*E6, E7, E6 etc*).

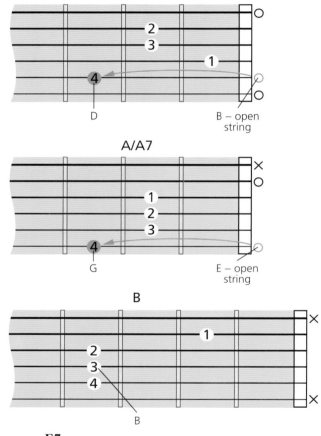

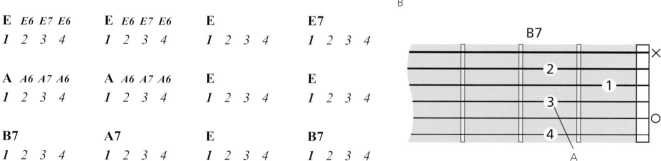

E *E6 E7 E6*	**E** *E6 E7 E6*	**E**	**E7**
1 2 3 4	*1 2 3 4*	*1 2 3 4*	*1 2 3 4*
A *A6 A7 A6*	**A** *A6 A7 A6*	**E**	**E**
1 2 3 4	*1 2 3 4*	*1 2 3 4*	*1 2 3 4*
B7	**A7**	**E**	**B7**
1 2 3 4	*1 2 3 4*	*1 2 3 4*	*1 2 3 4*

As you can hear, dropping the pitch from G to E adds richness and resonance; and it will also enable us to make some further embellishments to our 12-bar. The photographs on the right show how the

basic E/E7 and A/A7 shapes can be enhanced with extra notes similar to those in the riffs on the last two pages, producing so-called '6th' chords that provide an effective link between the straight majors

Right and below:

(Right) An E6 chord (see italics in exercise). This shape, a 'regular' E major with an extra note supplied by the little finger on the 2nd string/2nd fret, forms a useful musical bridge between E and the E7 chord illustrated in the left-hand photograph below.

Above and left: Like E6, A6 (above) is a transitional chord. It's created by adding the little finger to the 1st string/2nd fret; from here, the 'pinkie' can slide upwards to the 3rd fret to produce an A7, as shown in the picture on the left.

and 'dom 7s'. Mastering the major/6th/7th progressions (which should be deployed in bars 1, 2, 5, and 6 of the blues, as indicated by the italicized letters) may be something of a challenge to your 'pinkie', which has to move steadily up the 2nd and 1st strings to reach the required notes – but the pleasing results will certainly justify the effort!

8-Bar Shuffle

The words '12-bar' and 'blues' may seem synonymous, but real-life blues performers often deviate from the 'textbook' verse structure we've been experimenting with so far.

Some singers and players on the very earliest blues recordings, made in the 1920s and 30s, rarely (if ever) used regular chord changes or predictable verse-lengths – an approach frequently shared by later stars such as John Lee Hooker. There are also many classic blues numbers, old and new, in 8- or 16-bar forms; and top present-day performers constantly refresh and enliven the music's traditional roots by adding fresh harmonies and unexpected rhythmic twists to their songs.

The blues we'll be working on for the rest of this chapter incorporates a few of these 'special features'. It is eight bars long, contains some modified chords (though most of these are similar to ones you've already encountered), and is based around a 'shuffle' rhythm that will soon be giving your plectrum rather more to do than straight strumming. However, we'll start, as usual, with your fretting hand: here are the basic shapes it needs for this piece.

A 'trio' of 'dom 7s'

The D7 shown below should be familiar from pages 38-41, while the other two chords are slightly different-sounding versions of the A7 and E7 fingerings that appeared in the last exercise. All three shapes are pretty simple – but be warned that we'll be making some variations to them a little later on! For now, though, try them out in the sequence at the bottom of page 45, using a single plectrum stroke on

Above: The new A7 chord (also seen in the diagram opposite). It contains no less than three open-string notes – from the 1st, 3rd and 5th strings – and has a noticeably more resonant sound than the A7 you learned on pages 42-3.

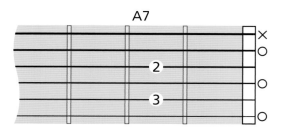

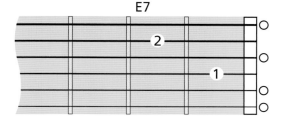

Above: The D7 shape for this 8-bar blues is exactly the same as the one you used previously.

Left: This E7, like the A7 on page 44, is full of open strings, and may make the floor shake if you play it on an electric!

each beat of its eight bars. Like a 12-bar blues, the cycle can either be endlessly repeated (until you – or your neighbours – have had enough of it!) or concluded with a single A7 chord after bar 8.

A7	**A7**	**D7**	**A7**
1 2 *3* 4	*1* 2 *3* 4	*1* 2 *3* 4	*1* 2 *3* 4
E7	**D7**	**A7**	**E7**
1 2 *3* 4	*1* 2 *3* 4	*1* 2 *3* 4	*1* 2 *3* 4

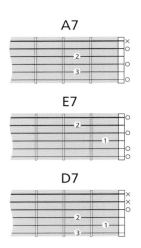

It's time to make the title of this exercise a reality by turning our 8-bar blues into a 'shuffle'. The theory behind this irresistible rhythm may seem a little daunting, but you'll find that actually playing it soon becomes second nature – especially as you're likely to recognize its distinctive 'feel' from countless blues and pop records.

All our preceding blues exercises have been built up from bars with four beats (*1-2-3-4*). The shuffle retains these, but **subdivides** each beat into **three**. To get the idea of how this works, count '*1-2-3-4*' a few times, then break up the beats by calling out '**1**,*2,3*– *2,2,3*–*3,2,3*–*4,2,3*.' (You must obviously fit the subdivided 'triplets' into the four main beats without changing speed.) Once you're able to count or clap the shuffle rhythm, take up your guitar, select a six-string shape such as the E7 you've just learned, and strum on all twelve of the shuffle subdivisions, stamping your foot or speaking the beat numbers to keep in time. Continue your 'shuffling' on A7 and D7, making sure that your busy plectrum doesn't accidentally strike their 'silent' strings.

After a few minutes' vigorous chording, you may find that your picking hand is beginning to tire. A good way of reducing muscle fatigue, and cutting down on excess hand and wrist movement, is to alternate between downward and upward plectrum strokes when playing shuffle rhythms (see photographs). At first, you may find the upward strums hard to control; keep practising until you can produce chords of exactly the same volume and texture, whatever the direction of your plectrum.

Cutting back on your strums

While mastering the shuffle, you've been clocking up an impressive tally of 12 chords per bar, so you may be relieved to know that in our 8-bar blues, you'll be playing on only the **first** and **third** subdivisions of each beat. The exercise below will help you to do this; count out the rhythm displayed beneath the chord letters as you try it, but don't strum on the bracketed '2s'. The *d* and *u* symbols indicate down- and upstrokes.

Above: A reminder of the three chord fingerings you'll be using for the 'shuffle' exercise below.

A7				**D7**			
1-*(2)-3*	2-*(2)-3*	3-*(2)-3*	4-*(2)-3*	**1**-*(2)-3*	2-*(2)-3*	3-*(2)-3*	4-*(2)-3*
d	*u d*	*u d*	*u d u*	*d*	*u d (etc.)*		

E7				**A7**			
1-*(2)-3*	2-*(2)-3*	3-*(2)-3*	4-*(2)-3*	**1**-*(2)-3*	2-*(2)-3*	3-*(2)-3*	4-*(2)-3*

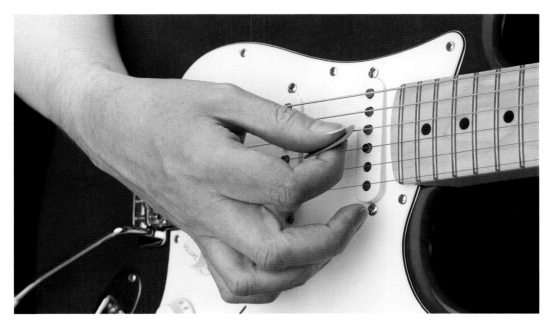

Left: Starting a downstroke on a D7 chord; the 5th and 6th strings remain silent.

46

Above: Alternating between down- and upstrokes with your plectrum is an efficient way of picking chords in swift succession.

Below: Don't allow your right wrist to tense up during busy strumming passages like the ones in this exercise.

Above: When strumming, let the plectrum skim across the top of the strings for a smoother sound.

In a moment, it'll be time to combine your shuffle chords with a simple lead guitar line in a full blues cycle. First, though, let's take a closer look at the unnamed, asterisked shapes in bars 1 and 5 of the tablature at the top of page 49 (this numbering excludes the opening single-beat bar). The first is an A7-type fingering, shifted a fret down from its normal position; the second is a similarly displaced D7. They're both 'passing chords', played for a single plectrum stroke before the regular A7 and D7 shapes from which they're derived, and they generate a 'slithery' harmonic effect that's a blues guitar stock-in-trade. After striking them (they both fall on upstrokes), simply slide your left-hand fingers up the fretboard to the main A7 and D7, as demonstrated in the pictures above and opposite.

When tackling the **accompaniment** for our 8-bar blues, count out a bar of silence ('**1**,*2,3*–*2,2,3*–*3,2,3*–*4,2,3*') before beginning to play. The last beat of this ('*4,2,3*') corresponds to the short measure at the start of the tablature, for which there's no

backing; the first chord you strike (A7) is a downstroke on beat 1 of the piece's first full bar. Play only on the first and third subdivisions of the beats (as indicated by the numbers beneath the stave), alternating between down- and upstrokes as you did on the previous exercise.

Adding a tune

The **melody line** for the blues forms a separate part, notated on the 'tab'. It uses only the top three strings, and its notes are positioned over the beats/subdivisions on which they should be played. When practising the melody without accompaniment (try this very slowly at first!), count '**1**,*2,3*–*2,2,3*–*3,2,3*', then play the three notes of the short opening bar on beat **4**.

As with *Amazing Grace*, you'll get the most from this exercise if you record the chordal backing (preceded by your count-in) and then solo 'live' over the top of it – or if a fellow-guitarist can be persuaded to accompany you.

Above: The mutated A7 shape featured in bar 1 of the exercise and described in the text. It's simply a standard A7 with the notes on its 4th and 2nd strings slid one fret down.

Opposite: The shuffle chords are the bedrock of this exercise – make sure you can play them evenly, using down- and upstrokes as before.

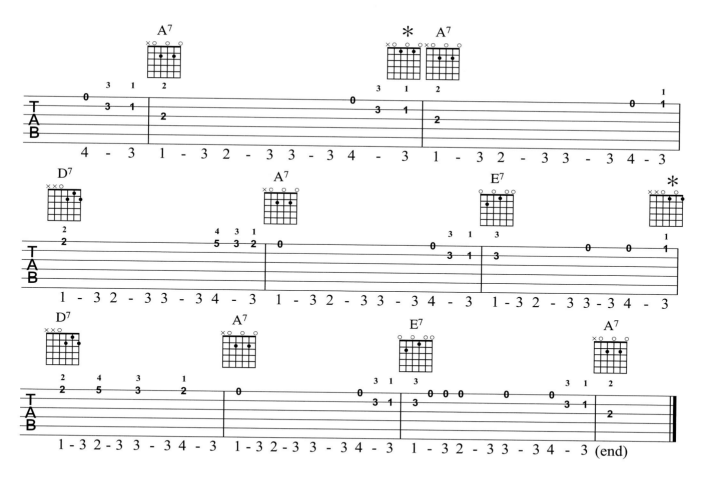

Chapter 4

The Right Hand

There are many possible methods of modifying or 'personalizing' your guitar sound, some of them requiring the purchase of hundreds or even thousands of pounds worth of customized instruments and ancillary gear. However, one small, highly significant change you can make immediately will cost you nothing – in fact, it could actually save you money, as it involves putting aside your plectrum and striking the strings with your bare fingers or nails instead. Doing this not only transforms your tone; it brings previously unreachable combinations of notes and chords under your right hand, and allows you to create smooth, rippling rhythmical patterns that will sound especially good when accompanying singers and other instrumentalists. Follow the instructions on the next few pages to get the feel of so-called 'fingerstyle' playing, which, as you'll soon discover, can also be used in combination with conventional flatpicking…

Plectrum or Fingers?

For pounding out chords, as you've been doing for much of the last chapter, or for strident soloing, the plectrum is an ideal playing tool. It produces a uniquely crisp, percussive sound, saves your striking hand from the potentially damaging effects of repeated, high-velocity scraping against the guitar's strings – and, if it splits or wears down, can be replaced instantly, unlike a sore fingertip or a broken nail.

Despite all this, numerous electric and acoustic performers choose not to use it. Flat-picks are anathema to classical and flamenco guitarists, whose nylon-strung instruments are specifically designed for 'fingerstyle' techniques; while some jazz and rock axemen consider that the plectrum spoils their touch, and prefer to make direct contact with the strings. Among their number are Mark Knopfler of Dire Straits, and British rhythm-&-blues veteran Wilko Johnson, who protects his bare right-hand fingers with a coating of industrial adhesive before going on stage! For other musicians, though, the problem with the plectrum is simply that it stops them reaching the notes they need: its inability to strike non-adjacent groups of strings simultaneously can make rippling, folk-type accompaniments difficult, and more elaborate guitar parts quite impossible, without resorting to fingers and nails.

This chapter provides a brief introduction to fingerstyle, and also looks at some of the ways in which your right-hand digits can work in tandem with the plectrum to extend its range and capabilities. Before we get started, however, you need to make sure that your nails are in good shape for the task ahead. Trim them to the lengths shown in the photograph opposite, and make sure there are no jagged or uneven edges that can catch or tear on the strings. Some players cut their right-hand nails almost as

short as those on their left hands, and pick with the fleshy tips of their fingers, but this method often generates a sound lacking volume and 'bite', and is more likely to lead to inflammation and discomfort than the combination of nail and tip preferred by most fingerstylists.

Below: The nails should extend slightly beyond the tips of the first, second and third fingers for 'fingerstyle' playing. The thumbnail can be kept a little longer.

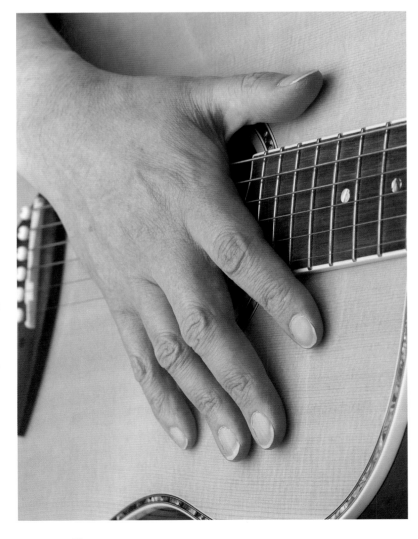

Basic Fingerpicking

When preparing to play fingerstyle, position your right hand as shown in the photograph, resting your thumb on the guitar's 6th string, and your index, middle and ring fingers on the 3rd, 2nd and 1st. We won't be using the little finger, though it does feature in some specialized flamenco techniques.

Your thumb's main task is to pick out bass notes from the three bottom strings; it rarely strums, and, for obvious reasons, only ever produces downward strokes. Each of the other three digits is effectively 'in charge' of the string it currently occupies, and will usually pick it in an upward, clawing movement – though the index (sometimes joined by other fingers) can also 'brush' across groups of strings, rather like a plectrum.

Form a chord of G (see diagram), and sound the 6th string with your thumb; while it's ringing, strike the 3rd, 2nd and 1st strings one after the other, using the individual fingers assigned to them; finally, strum the top three strings quickly with the edge of the nail on your index. (Don't touch the 5th and 4th strings.) Practise picking clearly and smoothly, and ensure that you don't dampen any vibrating strings with your wrist or a stray finger. After getting used to the sensation of playing without a plectrum, make things more rhythmical by counting out two bars of four slow beats, and synchronizing your picking and strumming with them as follows – adding a new note (an open D, struck by your thumb) at the start of bar 2:

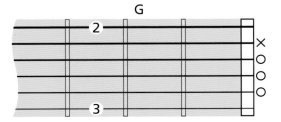

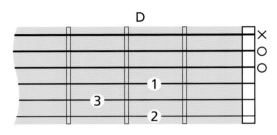

Below: This picture shows the optimum angle for your right-hand fingers and thumb on the strings, prior to picking.

Bar 1: (G shape)

Pick 6th string (G)	Pick 3rd string (G)	Pick 2nd string (B)	Pick 1st string (G)
1	*2*	*3*	*4*

Bar 2: (D shape)

Pick 4th string (D)		Strum top 3 strings	
1	*2*	*3*	*4*

Repeat this pattern, gradually building up speed, and then try combining it with a similar two-bar figure, based on a D shape.

Bar 1: (D shape)

Pick 4th string (D)	Pick 3rd string (A)	Pick 2nd string (D)	Pick 1st string (F# – i.e. F sharp)
1	*2*	*3*	*4*

Bar 2: (D shape)

Pick 5th string (A)		Strum top 3 strings	
1	*2*	*3*	*4*

Broken Chords

So-called **broken chords** like these, with their gently see-sawing bass notes, are a perennial favourite with country and folk-style pickers – and in a moment, you will be learning a little more about these musicians' fingerstyle methods.

Below: After you've sounded the strings, make sure your fingers and wrist don't muffle the notes and chords you've generated.

Right: Here, the thumb has just struck the 6th string; the other fingers are ready to play the 3rd, 2nd and 1st.

Picking and Hammering-On

The right-hand technique you've just been shown works well on many other chords, but is especially effective when one or both of their alternating bass notes comes from an open string.

Here's how fingerpicking can be used with the shapes for A and E:

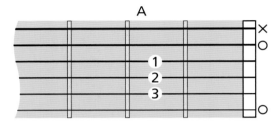

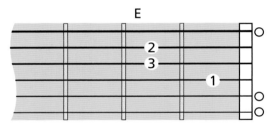

Bar 1 (A shape):

Pick 5th string (A)	Pick 3rd string (A)	Pick 2nd string (C#)	Pick 1st string (E)
1	*2*	*3*	*4*

Bar 2 (A shape):

Pick 4th string (E)		Strum top three strings	
1	*2*	*3*	*4*

Bar 3 (E shape):

Pick 6th string (E)	Pick 3rd string (G#)	Pick 2nd string (B)	Pick 1st string (E)
1	*2*	*3*	*4*

Bar 4 (E shape):

Pick 5th string (B)		Strum top three strings	
1	*2*	*3*	*4*

(Go back to bar 1, or finish with a strummed A chord)

We're now going to add another element to our 'rippling' pattern by playing one bass note in each of the two chords as a 'hammer-on'. This involves picking a string, and then generating a second note from it *without another right-hand fingerstroke*. Try this by sounding an open D on the 4th string with your right-hand thumb. Immediately after striking it, bring your left-hand index finger down onto the same string at the 2nd fret, using a little more force than normal. The energy from your initial thumbstroke, plus the impact from depressing the string, should be

Top: The left-hand index finger poised to 'hammer-on' to the 4th string at the 2nd fret, as described here.

enough to produce a ringing 'hammered-on' E at the 4th string/2nd fret.

You can also 'hammer' the 5th (A) string on the 2nd fret with your second finger to create an unpicked B – and after a little practice, you'll be able to combine both the D/E and A/B hammer-ons with the A and E chords in the revised exercise below. Wherever you see its **H/O** instruction, execute a hammer-on at the start of the first beat, while keeping the other notes you're fingering held down as normal (see photographs).

Bar 1 (A shape):

Pick 5th string (A)	Pick 3rd string (A)	Pick 2nd string (C#)	Pick 1st string (E)
1	*2*	*3*	*4*

Bar 2 (A shape):

H/O 4th string D/E		Strum top three strings	
1	*2*	*3*	*4*

Bar 3 (E shape):

Pick 6th string (E)	Pick 3rd string (G#)	Pick 2nd string (B)	Pick 1st string (E)
1	*2*	*3*	*4*

Bar 4 (E shape):

H/O 5th string A/B		Strum top three strings	
1	*2*	*3*	*4*

(Go back to bar 1, or finish with a strummed A chord)

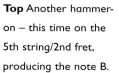

Top Another hammer-on – this time on the 5th string/2nd fret, producing the note B.

Below: Hammering on at the 4th string/2nd fret while holding down an A shape. (Despite appearances, the little finger does not touch the 1st string!)

Once you've mastered this, see how many more shapes you can link together and modify with hammer-ons!

Above: The right-hand position for the A shape hammer-on (opposite).

Playing in Sixths

As we've just seen, fingerstyle is good for rich-sounding, multi-string chords; however, it's also useful when we want to play just pairs of notes, allowing us to produce the pitches we require with almost any combination of strings.

One of the most attractive and effective of all two-note groupings are **sixths**, so-called because they're separated by six note-names. Since the distance between the open 3rd and 1st, and 4th and 2nd strings is itself a sixth (the string-to-string sequence of notes is **G**-a-b-c-d-**E** [3rd/1st] and **D**-e-f-g-a-**B** [4th/2nd]), it's particularly easy to obtain this pleasing interval from them – though it wouldn't normally be possible to do so with a plectrum, as the intervening 2nd or 3rd strings would get in its way.

The 'tab'-notated exercise below conveys the musical flavour of the sixth. There's no indicated rhythm, so you can linger over the notes for as long as you like. Use your right-hand thumb to strike the 4th string, and your index, middle and ring fingers for the 3rd, 2nd and 1st. Left-hand fingerings are given by the numbers above the stave.

Left: The second 6th interval in bar **1** of the first exercise. The second and third fingers hold down (respectively) the 4th and 2nd strings at the 2nd fret; the index is in place on the 3rd string/1st fret for the next fingered note.

Left: Fingering for the second pair of notes in bar **2** below. The third finger presses down the 1st string at the 4th fret, and the resultant note is combined with the open 2nd string. The second finger 'floats' above the fretboard.

Far left: The first note grouping for bar **3** in the exercise above, played on the 2nd and 4th strings.

Left: Back to the 2nd fret for the last chord in bar 3 above.

Playing these sixths doesn't put very heavy demands on the resources of your right hand – or, indeed, the resources of the guitar. In fact, you have more than enough spare finger and string capacity to add a supporting bass-line to the notes you're already picking! Try doing this now: the task is easier than it might seem, as all the extra notes beneath the sixths come from open strings – though you will have to alter your right-hand fingerings as shown on the following tablature.

Left: Second exercise – this fingering (for bar 1, second pair and bar 3, third pair) is combined with an open 5th string.

Below: The last note of exercise 2, fretted by the second finger on the 4th string/2nd fret, while the open 6th and 2nd string continue to ring.

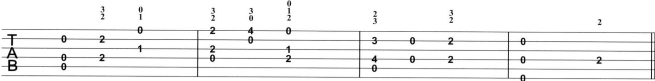

Picking Tricks

There are many other easy-to-reach sixth intervals on the guitar fretboard –
some of which will be featured in Chapter 5. In the meantime, let's return to
the ones you've just played, and try out an alternative – and rather
surprising – right-hand fingering method for them.

As you know, the plectrum's biggest handicap is its inability to sound non-adjacent strings at the same time. However, we can sometimes get around this by using it in *combination* with one of your right-hand digits. Hold your plectrum between your thumb and index as normal, place it behind the 4th string, and then move your second finger into position to pick the 2nd string (see photographs). The plectrum and finger will now be able to play the 4th/2nd-string pairing that starts our 'sixths' exercise, and to move up to the 3rd/1st strings for the other notes.

This technique is handy, but has obvious limitations, and a more versatile way of striking the strings with your fingers while retaining some of the hard, crisp attack associated with a plectrum is to use **fingerpicks**. These plastic or metal attachments, worn on your right-hand fingers and thumb, create much greater tonal power than nails and flesh – although many guitarists find them uncomfortable, and prefer simply to switch between standard fingerstyle and plectrum-based playing as necessary, accepting the inevitable differences in their sounds.

Above: A standard downstroke, with the plectrum about to play the 4th string.

Right: Using the plectrum in tandem with your second finger allows you to pick two strings at once.

Damping the strings

Your picking hand can also **damp** the strings. This works best when you strike single notes or chords with a plectrum while resting your wrist in front of the guitar's bridge, so that it just touches the strings. The results – slightly muffled, but preserving a little of the notes' original 'ring' – will be familiar from many pop records, but you may have to experiment to get the wrist pressure just right.

Less common ways of producing novel sounds from your strings include the use of various hand-held electronic devices. The most famous of these is the 'EBow', which can generate endlessly sustained notes and other effects, and is favoured by stars such as Eddie Van Halen, and The Edge from U2.

Above left: The plectrum and second finger sound the last pair of notes in bar one of the exercise.

Below left: The exercise's left-hand fingerings (like this one, for the end of bars 1 and 2) are unchanged.

Left: The 2nd and 1st strings picked by the plectrum/second finger combination.

Below: Fingerpicks produce a more robust sound than nails – but they don't suit some players.

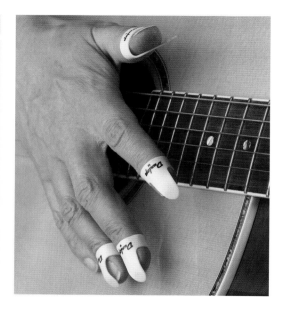

Chapter 5

Exploring the Neck

The notes and chords you've mastered so far have all been
played on your instrument's open strings, or at its lowest five fret
positions — and, for simple parts and elementary harmonies,
there's often no need to stray much further up the neck.
However, most acoustic guitars have a minimum of 14 frets 'clear
of the body' and easily accessible by your left hand, while electric
axes, with their deep cutaways, allow you to reach an even
longer expanse of fingerboard. What's it there for? And how
can you learn to make proper use of it?

Some of the answers to these questions are fairly
straightforward. The upper frets supply higher pitched notes,
as well as giving access to harmonics, the distinctive, bell-like
overtones you'll be experimenting with a little later. But the neck
also holds other musical possibilities, and this chapter aims to
unlock the secrets of its initially daunting expanse of wood
and metal, and to show you how to begin finding your
way around it.

Scarborough Fair

On the next six pages, you're going to be learning how to play and accompany the English folk song Scarborough Fair *in several different ways – a process that will soon be taking you to areas of the guitar's fingerboard you haven't visited before. For the moment, though, let's stay in the lower fret positions, as you practise the basic notes and harmonies for the piece.*

Five of the six chords you need have been used in previous exercises, and as you can see, the sole new shape is much simpler to finger than its strange name – B7sus4 – might suggest!

A classic song

Since you probably know the tune for *Scarborough Fair* (which has a three-beat pulse, like *Amazing Grace*), try singing or humming it with the chords straight away.

Em

B7

Below: You can accompany *Scarborough Fair* using a plectrum…

A

G

Opposite: …or you can try using fingerstyle techniques on its six different chords, whose shapes are shown here.

D

B7sus4

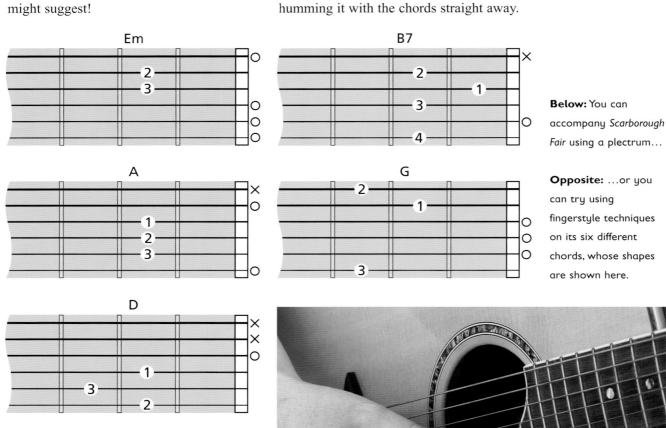

The song is quiet and gentle, so you might want to strum only on the first beat of each bar. Alternatively, you could experiment with some of the rippling fingerpicking techniques we explored in the previous chapter, using your right-hand thumb to sound the root note of every chord (these are identified above the diagrams on the previous page) before striking the higher strings with your other digits.

Em			Em			D			Em		
Are	-	you	go-	ing	to	Scar-	bo-	rough	Fair?	-	-
1	*2*	*3*	*1*	*2*	*3*	*1*	*2*	*3*	*1*	*2*	*3*

Em			Em			A			B7sus4		
Par-	-	sley,	sage,	-	rose-	ma-	ry	and	thyme;	-	-
1	*2*	*3*	*1*	*2*	*3*	*1*	*2*	*3*	*1*	*2*	*3*

B7		
-	-	Re-
1	*2*	*3*

Em			G			G			D		
mem	-	ber	me	-	to	one	who	lives	there,	-	-
1	*2*	*3*	*1*	*2*	*3*	*1*	*2*	*3*	*1*	*2*	*3*

Em			Em			D			Em		
She	-	once	was	a	true	lo-	ver	of	mine.	-	-
1	*2*	*3*	*1*	*2*	*3*	*1*	*2*	*3*	*1*	*2*	*3*

The tune-and-chords 'tab' for *Scarborough Fair* shown below will enable you to play the melody line solo (left-hand fingerings for it appear above the stave as usual) – or with accompaniment supplied by a friend or from a recording.

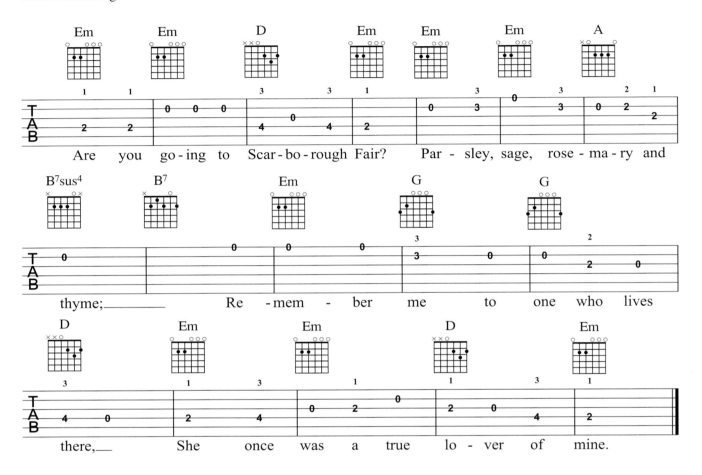

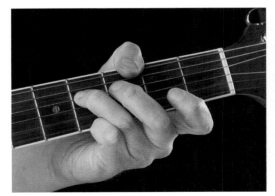

Above: The left-hand fingering for part 1a of *Scarborough Fair*, as shown on the tablature opposite.

Right: The two fretted notes for part 1b of *Scarborough Fair* come from the 2nd and 3rd frets on the 1st string.

66

Taking it higher

As you perform the song, you may feel that its overall sound, while pleasing, is rather murky and indistinct, with the melody sometimes in danger of being swamped by the chords. The best way to solve the problem is to raise the **pitch** of the tune, shifting it away from the part of the musical spectrum that it currently shares with the backing. To accomplish this, you need to move up the neck, and take advantage of the higher notes that only the 1st string can provide. However, abandoning the more familiar, lower frets can be unnerving, so we'll do it gradually, relating all new finger positions to the ones you know already.

To start the process, try playing the three fragments of *Scarborough Fair* displayed on the following tablature. Each appears in its original, lower-pitched version, then in the higher register that you'll shortly be using for the song's entire melody.

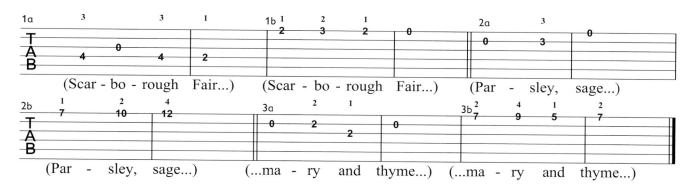

(Scar - bo - rough Fair...) (Scar - bo - rough Fair...) (Par - sley, sage...)

(Par - sley, sage...) (...ma - ry and thyme...) (...ma - ry and thyme...)

Top: Section 2b of the song: here, the index finger on the 1st string/7th fret provides the first note ('Par-'), and your second and fourth fingers must stretch out to (respectively) the 10th and 12th frets for '-sley' and 'sage.'

Left: '...ma-ry and thyme' (part 3b in the tablature). The first of the three notes comes from the 7th fret (second finger), the second from the 9th fret (fourth finger), and the third from the 5th fret (index) – all on the 1st string.

The three sections of *Scarborough Fair* featured on the previous pages may not make much musical sense on their own – but between them, they take in all but one of the notes required to play the tune at its new, raised pitch. (The sole exception is the D at the end of the word 'there' in the third line; this comes from the 2nd string/3rd fret, and you've used it many times before.) Having made your first venture up the neck, you're now ready to try the whole melody in its upper register version. Here it is, with all its fingerings.

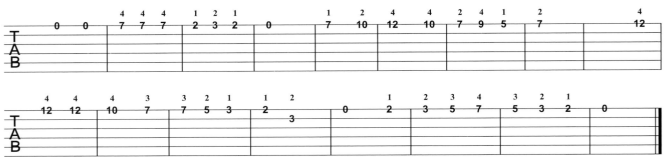

It's good to show off the guitar's high notes after spending so long on open strings and lower frets – but you may well have found the business of actually locating and moving between them rather a struggle. This isn't only due to unfamiliarity; because almost all the melody comes from the 1st string, your left hand has had to jump constantly up and down the fingerboard, reducing your speed and leading to mistakes. The solution is to master **position playing**, which involves finding as many as possible of the notes you need for tunes and licks in just one area

of the neck, and moving between adjacent strings instead of making time-consuming up-and-down left-hand leaps. Though position playing is beyond the scope of this book, you can get a taste of how to use other strings to support the 1st in the final *Scarborough Fair* exercise below. It uses sixths (see pages 58-61) and a few other easy intervals to produce a 'semi-harmonized' version of the melody; perform it fingerstyle, using your ring and index fingers on the 1st and 3rd strings, combined with your second and thumb where necessary.

Top: The sixth intervals shown in the tablature at the bottom of this page are all picked by the right-hand index and third fingers on the guitar's 3rd and 1st strings.

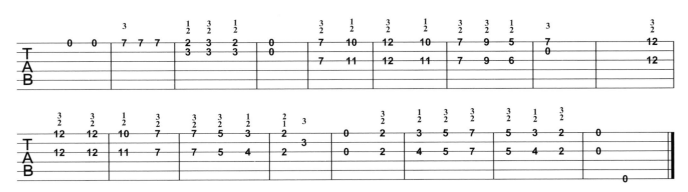

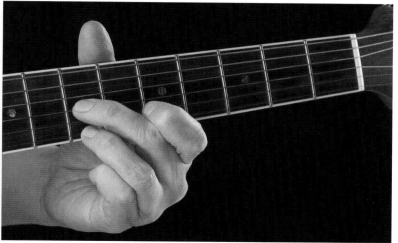

Above: Left-hand positions for the 'semi-harmonized' version of *Scarborough Fair* (bottom of page 68). This fingering gives you the 1st and 2nd string notes for the middle of bar 3.

Above right: These 7th fret notes occur at the start of bar 5.

Above: Up to the 12th fret for bar 6 ('sage') and bars 9-10 ('re-mem-ber').

Left: This familiar D chord shape is used in bar 13 ('there').

Open Strings and Shifted Shapes

We've seen how moving up the neck allows us to use the guitar's treble register for single or paired notes – but when we want to generate chords from its higher neck positions, things become more complicated.

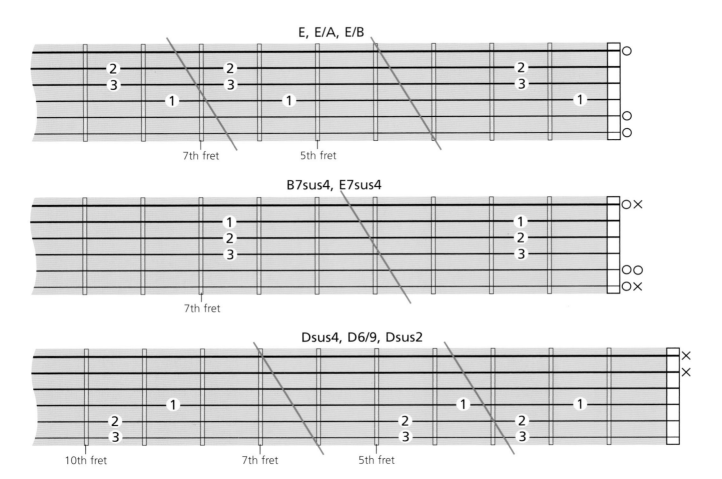

All the chords you've learned so far have been combinations of open and fretted strings, and we can take their fingered portions, like the 3rd, 4th and 5th string notes in the E shown above, and shift these freely around the fretboard to create new 'mini-shapes'. Try this by forming an E, sliding your three fretting fingers up to the 3rd and 4th frets (keeping their 'E-type' shape intact), and then picking the three strings you're holding down. They sound very similar to the original E, but slightly higher; in fact, the chord you're now playing is one of 'F sharp'. But strum all

six strings, and the result is musical chaos: the open Es and B on the 1st, 2nd and 6th haven't altered their pitches to match the three fingered notes, and now clash horribly with them.

Ringing the changes

Thankfully, this doesn't always happen. When you strike the strings after taking your E-type fingering to the 6th/7th, or 8th/9th frets (see diagram and photographs), the rich, jangling effect they produce is very enjoyable. Similarly pleasing combinations of open and fingered

70

Left: Shifting a standard 'E' fingering up two frets produces a partial chord of F sharp – but the clashing open strings surrounding it make the shape useless as a 6-string chord.

Left: However, moving the 'E' shape to the 6th and 7th frets (also see diagram opposite) creates a much more agreeable 'E/A' chord.

Below: Dsus2, played on the top three strings, fretted as shown here, combined with the open 4th.

notes can be made by shifting 'B7sus4' – first encountered in *Scarborough Fair* – and 'Dsus4' as illustrated. However, these chords, with their gently clashing, overlapping pitches, and mysterious, complex names, aren't needed nearly as frequently as 'bread-and-butter' 4-, 5- and 6-string majors and minors. To play these basic, essential harmonies further up the fingerboard, we need to adopt some radical and physically demanding new methods – as you're about to discover…

The Barré and the Capo

A 'fantasy' solution to our problem with open strings in higher-position chords would be to retune them to the various notes we need for different harmonies. This obviously isn't practicable, but we can do the next best thing, and alter their pitches by fretting – a method that inevitably involves adaptations to some of our left-hand shapes.

Let's begin by forming the simplified E major chord shown in the first photograph; you won't need the 5th or 6th strings, so hold down just the 3rd (with your second finger) and the 4th (with your third finger), combining them with the open 1st and 2nd. Next, slide your left-hand digits up a fret, and lay your index finger across the **1st and 2nd strings** at the 1st fret. Strike the new 4-string shape: assuming that your index can bear the strain of pressing down two strings simultaneously (doing this is known as **barréing**), you should be rewarded with a chord of F major, whose fingering pattern can also be shifted up the neck to provide other major chords.

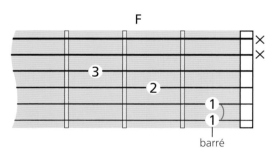

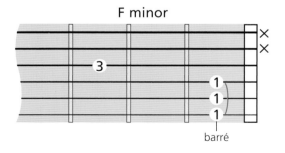

Other barréd chords

Barrés can be built into many left-hand shapes, enabling us to make *en bloc* changes to the pitch of formerly open strings. For example, the 4-string F minor in the diagram left is effectively a 'shifted' E minor, with its three upper notes barréd by the index instead of being left unfretted, and the 4th string held down at the 3rd fret. The barré can also be stretched across all six strings to provide 'full-size' chords in the higher positions (see photograph). However, many beginners find barrés hard to manage, and a more painless, though less flexible alternative to them is available in the form of the **capo** – a mechanical clamp that attaches across the neck, allowing 'open-string' shapes to be used wherever it's placed.

Above: This re-fingered E chord (substituting the second and third digits for the first and second) frees the left-hand index, which can be used to make a 'barré' when the shape is shifted up the neck.

Above left: Here, the second and third fingers have moved up to the 2nd and 3rd frets, while the index barrés across the top two strings. The result is a chord of F.

Above: A so-called 'great barré': the index presses down all six strings simultaneously, helping to make an F minor shape.

Left: Using a capo to create the same F minor chord produced with the great barré in the top right photo.

Harmonics

*We're going to finish this chapter by exploring a different way of generating notes and chords. It doesn't involve conventional fretting, but relies instead on the inherent physical properties of the guitar's strings, which are literally 'pressed into service' to create clear, ringing tones called **harmonics**.*

A string makes its sound though vibrations; but by touching it at specific places along its length, you can artificially 'divide' its vibrating length, and generate a 'harmonic' note higher than the one it's tuned to. Up to eight of these spots (known as **node points**) are accessible on each string, but we're going to focus on the most commonly used ones, located at the guitar's 12th, 7th and 5th frets (see diagram).

To play a harmonic, rest your left-hand index or second finger gently on the guitar's 6th string, directly above the metal of its 12th fret. Take your plectrum in your right hand, and pick the string; as soon as you strike it, move your left-hand finger clear. This momentary contact should produce a slightly 'disembodied', upper-register version of the E to which the string is tuned. The other five strings give

Left: Touching the 6th string at the guitar's 12th fret to generate a harmonic. Your left-hand finger should release the string just as the plectrum strikes.

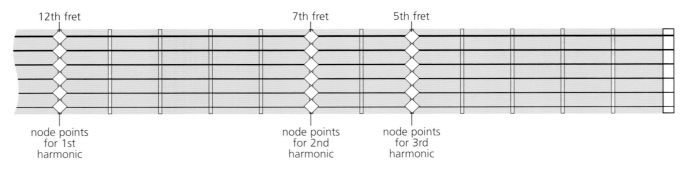

12th fret   7th fret   5th fret

node points for 1st harmonic   node points for 2nd harmonic   node points for 3rd harmonic

correspondingly pitched 'octave' harmonic notes at the 12th fret; try each in turn, and then see if you can pick the 3rd, 2nd and 1st strings together to make a harmonic chord of E minor.

These 12th fret pitches are the strings' **1st harmonics**. For their **2nd harmonics**, move to the 7th fret, and use the same 'touching' technique there. The result, surprisingly, is a set of notes five 'tones' *above* those from the 12th: the 6th and 1st E strings generate Bs (compare these to the unfretted B on the 2nd string), while the 5th, 4th, 3rd and 2nd provide, respectively, E, A, D and F sharp. You may find it a little harder to sound the **3rd harmonics** at the 5th fret; here, each string's harmonic is two **octaves** (a distance equivalent between the open E on the 6th and 1st string) above its unfretted 'fundamental' note.

Top: A 2nd harmonic is available at the 7th fret on the 5th string.

Above: The harmonic here is an E two octaves above the open 1st string.

75

Chapter 6

Doing It Better

Open a guitar magazine, or gaze through the window of any music store, and you'll be confronted with an impressive variety of electronic devices designed to make your instrument sound just like the heavily 'treated' axes you hear on records. Some of the most popular of these gadgets and gizmos are described and illustrated on the next few pages; they can be great fun, and many players find them hard to resist. However, if you decide to buy one, don't allow it to smother your own developing style and individuality: use it sparingly, and remember that it has 'bypass' and 'off' switches! This chapter also provides information about recording gear and hi-tech practice aids such as drum machines – but begins with instructions for making a simple, though immediately noticeable, upgrade to your instrument by giving it a new set of strings.

Time For New Strings?

*Since you bought your guitar, its strings will have been gradually
deteriorating – an inescapable process caused by moisture and grease from
your hands, and the rigours of being constantly stretched and struck.*

Replace them before they start sounding dull and looking discolored; the small cost of doing so will pay immediate dividends in improved tone and feel. Ask your local music store what sort of strings you should buy for your instrument; most popular string sets are **light gauge**, but various different formulations are produced for acoustic and electric guitars.

Begin the string-changing process by slackening off your old 6th string until it's loose enough to be removed from its machine head. Protect your eyes from its sharp end, and be careful not to prick your fingers on it. Next, detach the string from the instrument's body: on an acoustic, it's generally held inside the bridge by a wooden pin, which must be pulled up to release it; electrics normally use a 'threading' system that makes it easy to push loose strings out of their bridges or tailpieces.

Attach your new string to an acoustic by shoving its ball-end into the bridge hole that housed its predecessor, anchoring it with the pin. On an electric, feed the string into the bridge, tailpiece or body, pulling it through until its ball-end prevents it from moving any further. Thread its other end

Below: If your guitar's tone is starting to lose its sheen when you strum, you probably need new strings.

Above: Check with your local music store to ensure you buy the correct type and gauge of strings for your instrument.

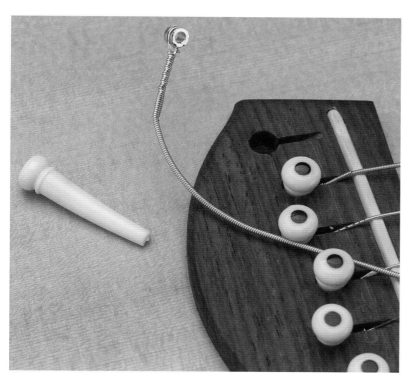

Left: Always replace strings one-by-one, to prevent sudden changes of tension that could damage the guitar's neck. They are easy to remove once they've been slackened off like this.

Below left: An acoustic guitar bridge with a pulled-out pin. The new string's ball-end is about to be inserted into the 'open' hole.

through the hole in the machine head's capstan, keeping the slack part of the string straight by placing the index finger of one hand on top of it. Now start turning the machine head's tuning key with your other hand, holding your 'guiding' index finger over the string until it's taut enough to stay in position by itself. Increase the tension

steadily, bringing the string up to its 'target' note; check this against a pitch pipe or similar device, and be prepared to retune almost immediately – it will take several minutes for the new string to settle down and hold its pitch properly. Trim its end with a pair of wirecutters, and then change the other five!

Above: After securing the string at the bridge, wind it onto the machine head, using a finger to keep it in place.

Electronic Aids

Most music stores boast a bewildering array of hi-tech guitar-related gadgets, but these can be separated into two basic categories: effects units that can modify the sound of your instrument (described in detail on pages 82-83), and equipment designed to guide you and enhance your playing as you practise, which we'll be focusing on first.

Perhaps the most basic of all practice aids is the humble **metronome** – once driven by clockwork, but now more commonly microchip-based and battery-powered. One of the hardest musical skills for budding guitarists to acquire is the ability to keep time. It's all too easy to rush ahead of the beat on easy chords, then slow up as you fumble for trickier fingerings, and the metronome's unyielding, clicking pulse

Left: The Yamaha ClickStation – a 21st-century metronome providing a wide range of rhythms. It even features a vibrating pad that supplies silent timekeeping pulses!

Left: Yamaha's Magicstomp unit offers electric guitarists up to **198** digital effects, including simulations and 'models' of a selection of classic amps, speakers and microphones.

can alert you to these deviations, and help you correct them.

However, its monotonous sound is less than inspiring, and you may prefer to play along to a **drum machine** instead. These usually require amplification, but can give reasonable results when plugged into the 'aux' sockets on your hi-fi or portable stereo (though excessive bass and volume settings may cause distortion and loudspeaker damage!) Even the cheapest models now provide a range of basic 4- and 3-beat rhythms, as well as jazz, Latin and other more exotic percussion parts, all with adjustable tempos. The patterns you select can be set to cycle endlessly, or you can programme them into 'songs' containing the exact number of bars you need.

For the ultimate in self-accompanying sophistication, there are ingenious (and often expensive) devices offering what's sometimes called a 'band in a box'. These build on the concept of the programmable drum machine, incorporating synthesized or sampled drum tracks, as well as simulated bass and (occasionally) rhythm guitar sounds. You set the length, speed and style of the song, enter the names of the chords it uses, then simply press 'play' and use the backing for your own solos!

Above: The Magicstomp's back panel incorporates mono and stereo outputs, plus a USB connector; its internal programs can be edited via computer, and upgraded with downloads from the manufacturer's website.

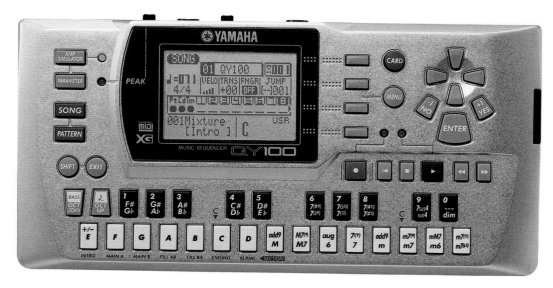

Left: The QY100 is described by its maker, Yamaha, as 'a palm-sized mini-studio, portable backup band and practice partner'. It can generate bass lines, chords and rhythms, and guitarists can plug their instruments directly into it and play through its built-in effects.

Most of the gear described on the last two pages will work alongside any instrument, but pedals and other sound-modifying devices require a direct feed of the signal from your guitar – so to use them, you need either an electric, or an acoustic with a pickup. You'll also have to buy at least one extra connecting cable, in order to plug your axe into the effects unit, and then link its output to your amplifier.

Pedal to the metal

The most popular 'stomp boxes', as effects pedals are sometimes known, include **distortion generators** that allow you to simulate stadium-style overdrive and 'fuzz'

at living-room volumes, and **wah-wahs** that apply sweeping boosts and cuts across the spectrum of audio frequencies emitted by your guitar. These, along with radical sound-reshapers such as **tremolos** (which create rapid fluctuations in level) and **aural exciters** (supercharged tone controls that give extra 'brightness' and 'edge'), are only suitable for fully-fledged electrics. However, other effects, like **chorusing** (a combination of delay and pitch shift that thickens the sonic texture and produces a distinctive 'swishing') and **reverberation** (echo), can be equally effective on an amplified acoustic, as can **equalizers** (these shape the tone-colours from your

Below: This inexpensive unit offers no less than 74 different effects, ten of which can be used at once. It also boasts a sampler and a simple drum machine.

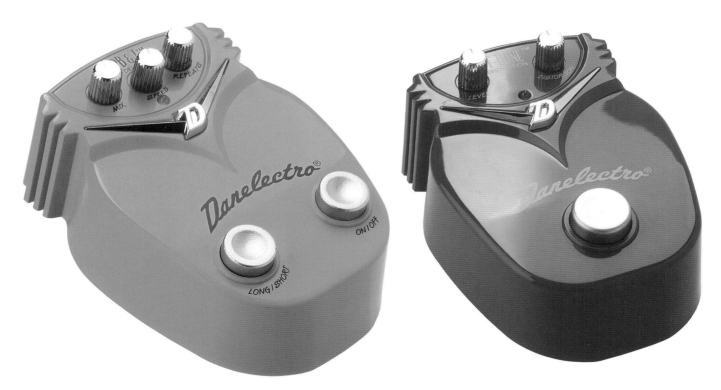

Above: Danelectro's 'slap echo' (short delay) and distortion pedals are part of a best-selling range of budget-priced, battery- or mains-powered 'stomp boxes'.

instrument's treble, bass and midrange), and **compressors** that 'tighten' the sound by reducing the difference between its loudest and quietest levels.

Devices like the ones mentioned above are all available separately, but for players wishing to use several at once, the most economical option is to buy a **multi-effects processor**. These compact units can provide a choice of 20 or more adjustable, combinable, microchip-generated effects, all of which can be activated, adjusted and combined as you choose. Some of the latest models also feature a CD input (for 'jamming' along to your favourite recordings), or even a built-in 'phrase trainer' – a digital sampler that can store licks and riffs you want to learn, and slow them down without changing their pitch, making it easier for you to master their individual notes.

Recording Your Guitar

A recording device of some kind – a cassette or MiniDisc machine, or perhaps, a basic, inexpensive multitracker – is an invaluable tool for anyone learning an instrument. Unlike friends or family, it never flatters or lies to you about how your playing really sounds; and, as we've seen in this book's earlier chapters, it can also serve as an ever-ready, ever-patient accompanist when you want to practise soloing over a chord sequence.

To get the best from your recorder, use it with a good-quality stereo microphone, or – for more serious, professional-style multitracking – a mono mic with a uni-directional field to minimize unwanted noise. It's also well worth investing in a robust, floor-standing mic stand with a boom attachment; this will save you considerable time and trouble when setting up your gear.

Recording an acoustic guitar is a tricky business, and, surprisingly, positioning your mic directly in front of the instrument's soundhole can lead to disappointing results; it's usually better to angle the mic slightly towards the bridge, or point it at the uppermost section of the fingerboard.

Experiment with both close and more distant placement: 'close-miking' gives a crisp, tight sound, though the powerful signals it generates may be hard to record without distortion (or the use of a compressor – see previous two pages). Moving the mic a few feet away reduces the overall level, but can introduce 'coloration' from stray room echoes.

Left: A robust, uni-directional mono microphone like the one shown here can be focused directly on your guitar, cutting out extraneous noises like traffic rumble.

Left: Moving your mic by only a few inches may have a radical effect on the overall sound it produces. A proper boom stand and clip will hold it steady and secure in any position that you choose.

Below: Portable MiniDisc recorders offer high-quality digital recording at affordable prices. For optimum results, keep such machines some distance from the mic — preferably on its 'dead' side, if it has one.

For an accurate, focused electric guitar timbre, start with the mic an inch or two away from your amp's loudspeaker cone. Make a test recording, keeping the amp volume and the mic level fairly low, then adjust as necessary, backing the mic away a little if the sound is coarse or overloaded. Unless you're using a recorder with a dedicated 'guitar' socket, don't attempt to plug your instrument directly into it: the output from the pickups is likely to be too strong, and the difference in **impedance** (electrical resistance) between axe and machine may spoil your tone.

Chapter 7

Taking It Further

At what stage can you truthfully say that you've become a 'real' guitarist? The answer largely depends on the level of skill you want to attain, and on how hard you're willing to work for it. However, having successfully reached the end of this book, you can now certainly claim to have mastered the basics of the instrument – and these final few pages are intended to whet your appetite for further practice and study by demonstrating some slightly more advanced 'tricks of the trade', and suggesting other ways in which you can continue to develop your technical and musical prowess.

The 'Sus4'

*For most of this book, we've concentrated on basic major and minor chords – but the next few pages feature a more advanced harmony, the **suspended 4th** – or 'sus4', in guitarists' jargon.*

To understand how 'suspensions' work, let's return to the song *Scarborough Fair* (where you first encountered a 'B7sus4' – see pages 64-65). Play a chord of E minor (you should know the fingering for it by now!), and sing or hum the first line, accompanying it on your guitar.

fourth step in the eight-note scale that begins and ends with D. However, you don't need to worry about scales or theory to enjoy the sound of the 'sus4' – or to realize how effective it can be when playing songs or tunes that have similar melodic contours to the opening of

Em	Em	D	Em
Are - you go- ing to		Scar- bo- rough Fair? -	-

You'll notice that the word 'Scarborough' uses two different pitches: the one for its first and third syllables matches the top note of your D chord, but the second one (on '-bo-') goes up a step, clashing very slightly with what you're playing. You can imitate this by fingering the two chords shown on the diagram below. Start by strumming the standard D shape (with your second finger fretting the 1st string as illustrated), then add your 'pinkie' at the 3rd fret/1st string for the '-bo-' of 'Scarborough', before releasing it again for '-rough'.

Scarborough Fair. Here are sus4 versions of a few other familiar chords; you'll be learning some more 'advanced' shapes – and putting them to effective musical use – in just a moment.

Opposite below:
Dsus4: use the illustrated fingering for the chord on the second syllable of 'Scarborough'.

C/Csus4

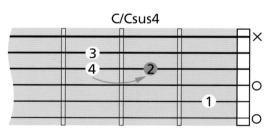

A/Asus4

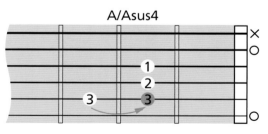

D/Dsus4

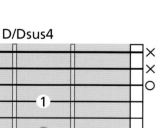

Sus4s in action

The '-bo-' chord is a suspended 4th: it gets its name because the 'new' note it contains (on the 3rd fret/1st string, replacing the one in the regular D major shape) is a G – the

F/Fsus4

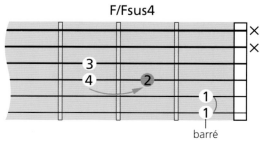

barré

Above: The E minor chord for the opening of *Scarborough Fair*.

Right: This D shape accompanies the first and last syllables of 'Scarborough'.

Amazing Grace Revisited

Our original version of Amazing Grace, on pages 30-35, used only simple harmonies and fingerings; let's return to it now, and try playing it rather differently, incorporating some of the harmonies and techniques featured in the last few chapters.

As you can see from the diagrams and tablature, we'll be introducing several new chords, including a couple of 'sus4s', to the song's backing. The first of these, Gsus4, occurs at the very start, and you should hold it for just one beat before returning to the standard G on beat 2, and moving to G7 (whose fingering you learned on pages 40-41), in the following bar:

Gsus4	G			G7	
A-	ma	-	zing	grace!...	
3	*1*	*2*	*3*	*1*	*2*...

The chords in bar 8 work very similarly, with Dsus4 occupying a single beat, and then giving way to a regular D major:

[bar 7]			*[bar 8]*		
D			Dsus4	D	
me!	-	-		I...	
1	*2*	*3*	*1*	*2*	*3*...

An unfamiliar, though very straightforward shape appears on the word 'wretch', and on the final 'now'. Officially named 'Cmaj7', it's easiest to think of it as a simple C (as used in bars 3 and 11) with its 2nd string left open, producing a jazzy clash that complements the tune and the surrounding chords. The only other new left-hand fingering is the somewhat 'churchy'-sounding D7 (for which the 1st and 6th strings remain silent) in bars 4 and 12.

Practise the chordal accompaniment to *Amazing Grace* on its own, then (if

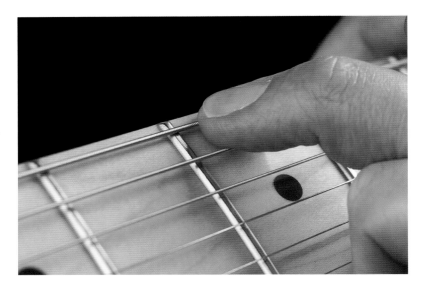

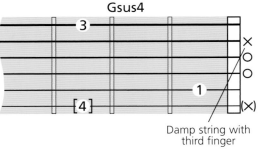

Gsus4

Above: Here, the third finger muffles the 5th string, which would otherwise create an unwanted clash in the Gsus4 shape shown on this page.

Damp string with third finger

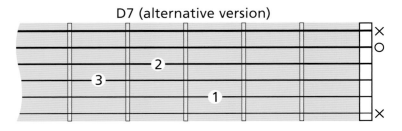

D7 (alternative version)

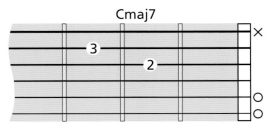

Cmaj7

possible) record it, and play the tape back as you rehearse the melody – which you're going to be performing entirely on harmonics! Follow the tablature to find the strings and fret locations you need for this; remember not to press down the required notes, but to touch and strike them as explained in Chapter 5. Good luck!

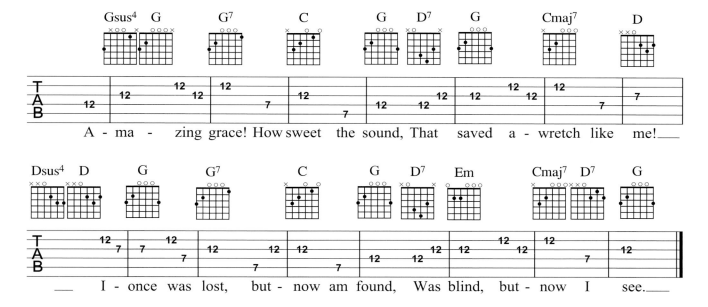

A - ma - zing grace! How sweet the sound, That saved a - wretch like me!___

___ I - once was lost, but - now am found, Was blind, but - now I see.___

Above: A four-string D7, featured in the accompaniment for bars 4 ('that') and 12 ('was') of *Amazing Grace.*

Above: Relying solely on harmonics to play a tune involves precise coordination between left and right hands.

Left: You may find that your harmonics ring out more clearly if you strike the strings a little closer to the bridge than normal.

And Finally...

We've seen how 'extended' harmonies like sus4s can work within chord sequences, but they're also widely used for embellishing the end of a blues cycle, and for providing a musical flourish at the conclusion of a song.

Though we explored a few elementary additions and substitutions to the basic, three-chord '12-bar' back in Chapter 3, we didn't make any changes to the so-called 'turnaround' – bars 11 and 12 of the blues, which lead back to the start of another verse, or on towards a final coda (or ending). In the key of A major, the 'prescribed' chords for the turnaround would simply be A or A7 (in bar 11), and E or E7 (in bar 12), but very few musicians would be content to settle for these! The diagram below sets out an alternative; as you can see, beats 2, 3 and 4 of bar 11 feature a three-note fingering which is shifted down the neck to form the changing chords.

Our 'sliding' shape begins as a partial A7, but as it moves downwards, it takes on different identities – and new, complex names that we won't go into here! However, progressions like this are a bedrock of blues style, and you'll be encountering many more of them in the future.

Alternative chords

We'll stay in A major to explore some flash-sounding replacements for standard majors or minors. These can provide a memorable finish to the numbers you play, and they're especially easy to finger in this key, thanks to the bass A on the guitar's

E⁷   D⁷   A⁷   (pic 1)   (pic 2)   (pic 3)   A⁷   E⁷   A

Left: Turnaround chords (see grids above) – picture 1: this A7 is played on the fretted 4th, 3rd and 2nd strings, with a bass note from the open 5th (A) string.

Right: Turnaround – picture 2: here, the preceding shape is simply shifted down by a single fret.

open 5th string. 'Set up' the first three by strumming an A followed by an E7 before trying each shape in turn.

A6

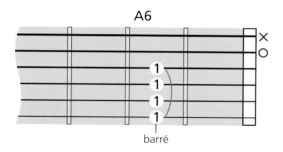

barré

• A6 will immediately remind you of The Beatles – the Fab Four ended several of their classic early hits with it.

• Our final 'closer', Am add9, is a piquant minor chord variant – precede it with a single E7.

A6/9

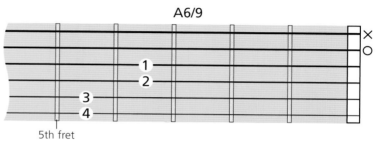

5th fret

• A6/9 is a richer version of the basic 6th chord, with a distinctively jazzy feel.

Asus2

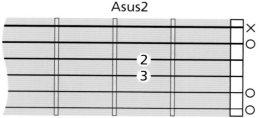

• Asus2 (a close cousin of the sus4 chord, with the second step in its associated scale 'suspended') provides a subtler, more restrained conclusion.

Am add9

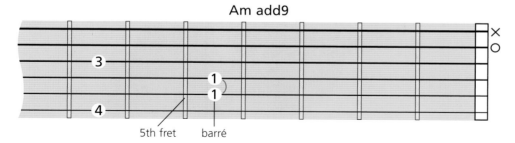

5th fret   barré

Above: Turnaround – picture 3: the final chord in our sequence lies yet another fret further down the neck.

Right: Master a few more shapes such as Am add9, and your playing will soon acquire a jazzy flavour!

The Next Step

This book has shown you some of the basics of guitar playing – but now you've reached its end, what resources do you need to help you make further progress? Here are some tips and suggestions…

Buy a chord dictionary

Knowledge of chords and their fingerings is vital for all guitarists. You've already mastered a handful of the most important shapes, but there are hundreds more to learn, and a comprehensive chord dictionary, with a strong binding to withstand years of heavy use, is an essential purchase.

Read 'the dots'

As you shop around for your chord dictionary, you'll notice that a number of intermediate and advanced guitar tuition books contain 5-line 'staff notation' as well as (or instead of) the tablature you've been using so far. Being able to decipher 'the dots', as they're often called, gives you access to a vast range of songs and other published material, and makes it easier for you to communicate with non-guitar playing musicians. One of the best introductions to notation is David Oakes' *Music Reading For Guitar* (Musicians' Institute).